Culpeper County, Virginia

DEEDS

Volume One, 1749–1755

Deed Book A, 1749–1753

and

Deed Book B, 1753–1756

— PAGES 1-364 —

Abstracted and Compiled

by

John Frederick Dorman

Heritage Books
2026

HERITAGE BOOKS
AN IMPRINT OF HERITAGE BOOKS, INC.

Books, CDs, and more—Worldwide

For our listing of thousands of titles see our website
at
www.HeritageBooks.com

A Facsimile Reprint
Published 2026 by
HERITAGE BOOKS, INC.
Publishing Division
5810 Ruatan Street
Berwyn Heights, MD 20740

International Standard Book Number
Paperbound: 978-0-7884-5068-6

Introduction

John Frederick Dorman III was a prolific genealogical researcher and author. In particular, the indexes he created for various county, city, and parish records have been of immense benefit to other genealogists.

County records often encompass a wealth of information, such as birth, marriage, death, land, probate, and court documents, which can be overwhelming to navigate without guidance. An index allows researchers to quickly locate the specific records they need by providing key details like names, dates, and locations, thus saving valuable time. Instead of sifting through hundreds or even thousands of handwritten pages, an index presents the relevant information up front, narrowing the scope of the search and enabling a more efficient review of records.

Indexes also simplify the process of searching across different types of records. County records are generally organized by document type and time period. Without an index, researchers would have to manually search through each category separately. Indexes eliminate this redundancy by allowing researchers to search for specific individuals or events across various record sets, which can provide a fuller picture of an individual's life and family connections.

Having access to well-organized indexes dramatically enhances the research process, improving both the efficiency and reliability of genealogical findings. For more than six decades John Frederick Dorman III worked to increase the depth of resources available to genealogical researchers, especially those who work in Virginia records. One doesn't even have to be a careful student in order to gain from his work. The careful student, however, can learn a great deal by studying his approach. Begin with his meticulous abstracts and even more meticulous indexes that go beyond names to places and subjects. Indexes and abstracts allow us to dig deeply into records and digging deeper into records means better research.

John Frederick Dorman

John Frederick Dorman (1928–2021) was the leading Virginia genealogical author of his era. His greatest accomplishment may have been as the editor and publisher of *The Virginia Genealogist* for fifty years (1957–2006); however, his role as editor of the fourth edition of *Adventures of Purse and Person*, summarizing in the three volumes all identified Virginia settlers prior to 1625 who left descendants, would be a close competitor.

His six major genealogical books on Virginia families (Robertson, Farish, Preston, Epes, Claiborne, and his unfinished Slaughter book) would alone be a remarkable legacy. However, in remembering him for these three major accomplishments, we must not forget the long list of articles which he wrote for the *National Genealogical Society Quarterly*, *The American Genealogist* and other journals, or his dozens of volumes of abstracts of Virginia county records and Revolutionary War pension applications.

Not merely a scholar and an author, Fred was deeply involved in the professional organizations of the genealogical world. He served the National Genealogical Society as a director for many years, and as an officer when needed. A founding member of the Board for Certification of Genealogists, he subsequently served as its president and later as executive director. He was a Fellow of the American Society of Genealogists (and later its president), and a Fellow of the Virginia Genealogical Society. A supporter of hereditary societies, he was a member of the Society of the Cincinnati in the State of Virginia, the Society of Colonial Wars (including service as Governor of the District of Columbia Society of Colonial Wars), the Sons of the American Revolution, Sons of the Revolution, Society of the War of 1812, and Jamestowne Society, among others.

Fred Dorman's abstracts of Virginia county records, remarkable for their detail and accuracy, were an important component in his impressive portfolio of genealogical books, and still as valuable to the researcher today as when he originally wrote them.

Pages 1-5. 15-17 April 1749. David Kinkead and Winifred his wife of St. Anne's Parish, Albemarle County, to William Duncan of St. Mark's Parish, Orange County. Lease and release; for £50 current money. 660 acres in St. Mark's Parish ... at the mouth of a branch of Kinkead's Run ... side of Besse Bell Mountain.
                              David Kinkead
                              Winifred Kinkead
   Wit: Saml. Scott, John Roberts Junr., Rowly (R) Duncan, Wm. (X) Duncan Junr.
   15 June 1749. Proved by Samuel Scott, John Roberts Junr., Rawly Duncan and William Duncan Junr.

Page 6. 18 May 1749. Bond of Henry Field as Sheriff of Culpeper County. For £1000 sterling. Securities, Robert Slaughter and Abraham Field of Culpeper County, Gent.
                              Henry Field
                              Robt. Slaughter
                              Abra: Field
   18 May 1749. Acknowledged.

Pages 7-12. 6-7 March 1748 [1749]. Mary Belfield, widow, John Belfield and William Jordan of Richmond County, Gent., executors of Thomas Wright Belfield, late of said county, Gent. to Richard Barnes, Gent., of said county. Lease and release; for £105 sterling. 1470 acres and water grist mill thereon erected, in St. Mark's Parish in the great fork of Rappahannock River ... 1000 acres, part whereof, was formerly purchased by Thomas Wright Belfield of Richard Maulden 25-26 May 1737, and 470 acres, the residue, was purchased by Thomas Wright Belfield of Elisha Perkins 7 Oct. 1734.
   Thomas Wright Belfield made his last will and testament 6 Dec. 1743 whereby he declares it to be his will that his executors should dispose of any lands they should think fit for the discharging of his debts, which will was proved in the County of Richmond. Thomas Wright Belfield departed this life greatly indebted and the executors in order to raise money for the paiment of his debts have contracted with Richard Barnes for the sale of land and water grist mill lying in Orange County.
                            John Belfield
                            W. Jordan
   Wit: Taverner Beale, Jas. Madison, Richard Scales, Edwd. (K) Rowland.
   20 July 1749. Proved by Taverner Neale, Richard Scales and Edward Rowland.

Pages 12-15. 20 July 1749. William Green of Culpeper County to Benjamin Thomas of King George County. Lease of 150 acres on a branch of Rappahannock called Hughes's River, part of 400 acres which was granted to William Duff, deceased, by patent and by William Duff conveyed to the late Robert Green and by Robert Green by his last will and testament bequeathed to William Green ... bounded on one side by the river and to

extend westerly so far as to include the house which is now
built thereon near the middle of the tract and to be laid off
in a long square the length of which shall not exceed three
times the breadth.

For the lives of Benjamin Thomas, his wife Katherine and
daughter Elizabeth.

Yearly rent, 530 pounds of tobacco on 1 January. If Benjamin
Thomas shall keep more than two tithables thereon besides himself in constant working, or three tithables if Benjamin Thomas
should not work himself, then to pay for each tithable above
the three 100 pounds of tobacco.

Benjamin will keep within a fence 100 apple trees, 100 peach
trees, and 25 cherry trees, safe from cattle, hoggs, sheep and
goats.   W. Green
                                          Benja. Thomas
   Wit: Joseph Watters, Robert Green, Duff Green.
   20 July 1749. Benjamin Thomas is to have the land this year
and the next ensuing rent free and for 1751 he is to pay 265
pounds of tobacco. I am to find him nails to build a tobacco
house.

                              W. Green
   20 July 1749. Acknowledged by William Green and Benjamin
Thomas.

Pages 15-17. 20 July 1749. William Poe and Lydia his wife of
Culpeper County to Cornelius Mitchel of same. For £8 current
money.   100 acres in the fork of the north branch of Rappahannock River ... corner of said Poe's land ...
                         William (W) Poe
                         Lydia (L) Poe
   20 July 1749. Acknowledged by William Poe and Lydia his wife.

Pages 18-21. 17-18 March 1748 [1749]. Daniel Brown and Frances
his wife of Orange County to John Brown of same. Lease and
release; for £45 current money.   150 acres in the Great Fork
of Rappa: River ... south side the south fork of the Gourd
Vine River between two cliffs on the river bank ... line of
the pattent granted to Richard Tutt Gent. to the first branch
...   Danll. Brown
                             Frances (F B) Brown
   Wit: P. Clayton, Richard Thomas, Eliza: Thomas.
   20 July 1749. Acknowledged by Daniel Brown and Frances his
wife.

Pages 21-23. 20 July 1749. James Pendleton and Elizabeth
his wife of Culpeper County to John Washburn of same. For 5
shillings.   269 acres on the north Little Fork of Rappa:
River ... said Pendleton's tract of land ... Cabbin Branch ...
Willis's line ... head of a valley corner to Francis Browning
... corner of said Washburn ...
                         Jas. Pendleton
                         Eliza: Pendleton
   20 July 1749. Acknowledged by James Pendleton and Elizabeth
his wife.

Pages 23-26. 20 July 1749. Thomas Washburn and Lucy his wife of Culpeper County to John Smith of same. In consideration of a tract of land on the north side of the north fork of Gourdvine River ... dividing line between Smith and Washburn ... down the meanders of the river ...

250 acres on the north side of the north fork of Gourdvine River being the upper part of a tract granted to Francis Browning for 430 acres 4 Feb. 1747 ... corner to Thomas Washburn and Nicholas Browning ... Duncan's line ... down the meanders of the river ...   Thomas (T) Washburn
                                        Lucy (L) Washburn
    20 July 1749. Acknowledged by Thomas Washburn and Lucy his wife.

Pages 26-28. 20 July 1749. John Smith of Culpeper County to Thomas Washburn of same. In consideration of a tract of land on the north side of the North fork of Gourdvine River being the upper part of a tract granted to Francis Browning for 430 acres which said upper tract Washburn purchased of Francis Browning ... corner between Thomas Washbourne and Nicholas Browning ... Duncan's line ... down the meanders of the river ... containing 250 acres.

Part of a tract granted to Goodrich Lightfoot 17 Sept. 1731 containing 86 acres ... dividing line between Smith and Washbourne ... down the meanders of the river.
                                        John (J) Smith
    20 July 1749. Acknowledged by John Smith.

Pages 29-32. 14-15 Aug. 1749. William Strother of St. Mark's Parish, Culpeper County, to William Pannell of same. Lease and release; for £250 current money. 392 acres in the Great fork of Rappahannock River on the north side of the north fork of Mountain Run ... south side of the north fork of Mountain Run ... by a branch ... part of a tract granted to Mr. Augustine Smith containing 4000 acres and sold by Smith to Richard Buckner and Colo. John Catlett ...
                                        Wm. Strother
    Wit: Anthony Strother, Thos. Covington, Roger Dixon.
    17 Aug. 1749. Acknowledged by William Strother. Mildred the wife of William Strother relinquished her right of dower.

Pages 32-35. 21 Sept. 1749. William Lobb and Catherine his wife of Culpeper County to Edward Dillard of same. For £14 current money. 100 acres on the Gourdvine Fork, part of a patent granted to William Lobb 10 Jan. 1735 [1736] ... the low grounds of the south fork of the Gourdvine River in or near the Revd. Mr. John Thompson's line on the north side thereof ... on a hill side ... up the river to Thompson's corner ... including the plantation whereon Edward Dillard now lives ...
                                        William Lobb
                                        Catherine (X) Lobb
    21 Sept. 1749. Acknowledged by William Lobb and Catherine his wife.

Pages 35-38. 7 Sept. 1749. Charles Dewitt Junr. of Culpeper

County to Frederick Fishback of same. For £16.2.6 current money. 50 acres, all that tract Charles Dewitt purchased of William Deatharidge within the Parish of St. Mark's ... on a rocky hill between the Beaverdamm Run and Indian Run ... head of a branch of Indian Run ... corner to Frederick Fishback's land ...

Chas: Dewitt

Wit: John Chisum, Harmon Holtsclaw, Joseph (X) Counce, John (X) Butten.

21 Sept. 1749. Proved by John Chisum, Harmon Holtsclaw, Joseph Counce and John Butten.

Pages 39-41. 21 Sept. 1749. Joseph Campbell and Sarah his wife of Culpeper County to Moses Botts of same. For £14.10.- current money. 127 acres in the Gourdvine Fork ... corner to Colo. Francis Thornton ... John Thompson's line ... by a branch ... to a gum on a hill ... as by deed from the Proprietor's Office 1 July 1749 ...

Joseph Campbell
Sarah (X) Campbell

21 Sept. 1749. Acknowledged by Joseph Campbell and Sarah his wife.

Pages 41-46. 20-21 Sept. 1749. Spencer Bobo of St. Mark's Parish, Culpeper County, planter, to Robert Terril of same, planter. Lease and release; for £50 current money. 400 acres in parish aforesaid being the land whereon Spencer Bobo now lives and did formerly belong to Henry Kendal and Thomas Walker and by them sold to Spencer Bobo ... at the mouth of Stony Run on the north side of Robinson River ... Adam Yager's line ... in a valley ... down the river ...

Spencer Bobo

Wit: John Nicholas, Thos. Slaughter, John Wynill Sanders.

21 Sept. 1749. Acknowledged by Spencer Bobo. Mary, the wife of Spencer, relinquished her right of dower.

Pages 46-50. 21-2[2] 7ber [Sept.] 1749. William Kirtlet of Culpeper County to Francis Kirtlet of same. Lease and release; for £30 current money. 614 acres ... at Rock Hall corner to Thomas Stanton... corner to Thomas Stanton and John Simpson ... down the Whitstone Rock Branch ... on the Stanton River ... corner to the said William Kirtlett ...

William Kirtley

Wit: William Tutt, G. Hume.

21 Sept. 1749. Acknowledged by William Kirtley. Sary, wife of William, relinquished her right of dower.

Pages 51-55. 19-20 Oct. 1747. Matthew Smith of St. Mark's Parish, Orange County, to Jacob Barler of same. Lease and release; for £20 current money. 200 acres taken off from 400 acres ... By pattent 24 June 1726 Matthew Smith is entitled to 400 acres in the first fork of the Rappadan River ... by a Beaver Branch of the Island Run ...

Matthew Smith

Wit: Herman (X) Bakmer, Adam (A Y) Jager, Stephen (X) Hernsberger.

21 Sept. 1749. Acknowledged by Matthew Smith.

Pages 55-58. 21 Sept. 1749. John Roberts of Culpeper County, Gent., and Elizabeth his wife to the Revd. John Thompson of same, Clerk. For £240 current money. 400 acres in the Fork of Rappahannock River which was granted John Roberts then of the Parish of St. George's in Spotsylvania County by pattent 30 June 1726 ... by the lower side of Flat Run ...
                              John (J) Roberts
                              Elizabeth (E) Roberts
   Wit: P. Clayton, Richard Young, Armistead Ball.
   21 Sept. 1749. Acknowledged by John Roberts and Elizabeth his wife.

Pages 59-64. 10 July 1749. John Roberts of St. Mark's Parish, Culpeper County, planter, to Richard Young of same, schoolmaster. Lease and release; for £24 current money. 300 acres part of a greater tract granted to John Roberts by pattent 18 June 1748 from the Honorable Thomas, Lord Fairfax's Office, for 589 acres ... in the little fork of Rappahannock River and on Little Battaile Run and the branches thereof ... north side little Battle Run ... line of the main patent which crosses the point of Little Battle Mountain ... it being the uppermost 300 acres.   John (J) Roberts
                              Elizabeth (E) Roberts
   Wit: John Thompson, Armistead Ball, Thos: Triplett.
   21 Sept. 1749. Acknowledged by John Roberts and Elizabeth the wife of John Roberts relinquished her right of dower.

Pages 65-68. 15 Aug. 1749. John Willis, the younger son of that name of Colo. Henry Willis, deceased, of Culpeper County, and Nanny his wife to Joseph Stevens of St. Margaret's Parish, Caroline County. For £107.10.- current money. 400 acres, formerly granted to Robert Spotswood, deceased, and by him deeded to John Willis ... on the north sides of Mountain Run and now joining to the lines of Colo. John Spotswood, Mr. Philip Clayton, James Pendleton and to a line of a tract formerly held by George Hoome known by the name of Fox Mountain Tract.   John Willis Junr.
                              Nanny Willis
   Wit: Anthony Strother, Roger Dixon, Thomas Slaughter, Thos. Covington.
   17 Aug. 1749. Acknowledged by John Willis Junr.
   2 Aug. [1749]. Commission to Robert Slaughter, Francis Slaughter, Philip Clayton and William Green to receive acknowledgment of Nanny, wife of John Willis.
   19 April 1750. Before the within commission came to hand Nanny Willis, wife of John Willis the Younger, was removed into Prince William County and we were informed that John Willis and Nanny his wife soon after removed out of this Colony.
                              Fras. Slaughter
                              P. Clayton

Pages 68-71 19 Oct. 1749. William Harris of Culpeper County to Richard Partridge of Westmoreland County. For £15 and a horse. 200 acres on Negro Run being part of a pattent granted to William Harris 30 May 1749 for 400 acres from the Proprietor's Office ... line of Charles Dewitt ... corner of John Button ... corner to Tilman Weaver, thence across William Harris's old line ...

William Harris

Wit: Matthew Partridge, John Boyer, Joseph (JM) Williams.
The within land mentioned was acknowledged in Orange County Court after an entry for the land and after the patten was taken the date of the deed was order than the patten and the parties thought the first deed in Orange Court was not sufficient and the parties have agreed that the deed acknowledged in Orange Court shall be void after the within deed is acknowledged.
19 Oct. 1749. Acknowledged by William Harris.

Pages 72-74. 19 Oct. 1749. William Harris of Culpeper County to John Boyer of Northumberland County. For £25 surrent money. 200 acres on Negro Run part of a patent granted to William Harris 30 May 1749 for 400 acres from the Proprietor's Office, one moiety being sold to Richard Patrridge of Westmoreland County and after Partridge's deed is laid off, then all the remainder of the patent.

William Harris

Wit: Matthew Partridge, Joseph (JM) Williams, Richard Partridge.
19 Oct. 1749. Acknowledged by William Harris.

Pages 74-77. 19 Oct. 1749. Thomas Kennerly and Mary Margarett his wife of Culpeper County to James Kennerly of same. For £20.8.- current money. 120 acres on the south side of the north fork of the Rush River ... north side of Thomas Kennerly's Delamore forest tract ... crossing the river ... part of a pattent granted to Thomas Kennerly and others for 1750.

Thos. Kennerly
Mary Margaret (X) Kennerly

19 Oct. 1749. Acknowledged by Thomas Kennerly and Mary Margaret his wife.

Pages 78-84. 25-26 Sept. 1749. Mosley Battaley of Spotsylvania County, Gent., and Elizabeth his wife to John Christopher of Orange County. Lease and release; for £50 sterling. 500 acres whereon Walter Fitzgerald the younger now lives in the first fork of the Rappadan River ... patent granted to said Elizabeth Battaley 28 March 1733 ...

M: Battaley
Elizabeth Battaley

Wit: Richard Bryan, Roger Dixon, Fran. Kirtley, H. Field, G. Hume.
19 Oct. 1749. Proved by Roger Dixon, Henry Field and George Hume.
4 Oct. [1749]. Commission to Robert Jackson, William Hunter, Fielding Lewis and Charles Dick, Gent., to receive the

acknowledgment of Elizabeth Battaley.
4 Oct. 1749. Elizabeth Battaley signified her consent to the conveyance.   Rob. Jackson
                                     William Hunter

Pages 84-89. 20-21 Dec. 1749. Daniel Brown and Frances his wife of Culpeper County to Rowland Cornelius of same. Lease and release; for £60 current money. 400 acres in the Gourd-vine Fork granted to Daniel Brown by a deed from the Proprietor's Office 28 Sept. 1748 ... line of a pattent granted to Robert Green ... on a ridge ... Robert Coleman's line ...
                                     Danl. Brown
                                  Frances Brown
    21 Dec. 1749. Acknowledged by Daniel Brown and Frances his wife.

Pages 89-93. 21-21 Sept. 1749. John Strother of St. Mark's Parish, Culpeper County, to William Covington of same. Lease and release; for £15 current money. 100 acres on the north side of the south fork of the Rush River ... near a branch on the side of Strother's corn field ... up the river ... corner to William Covington ... part of a tract granted John Strother containing 800 acres ...
                                  John Strother
    Wit: William Strother, Robert Covington, James Wade.
    18 Jan. 1749 [1750]. Acknowledged by John Strother.

Pages 93-98. 9-10 Oct. 1749. Goodrich Lightfoot of Culpeper County to Thomas Jones of same. Lease and release; for £65 current money. 246 acres in St. Mark's Parish ... corner of Mr. Joshua Fry ... with Richard Yarborough's line ... in a valley corner to John Willson ... south side of a branch ...
    100 acres on the south side of Robinson River where Mr. Joshua Fry's line crosses the river, formerly belonging to Richard Mauldin ... to Thomas Garrot's line ... to Ambrose Powell's line ... down the river ...
                                  Gr. Lightfoot
                               Susannah Lightfoot
    Wit: Jno. Bramham Junr., J. Bramham, Francis Cox.
    18 Jan. 1749 [1750]. Acknowledged by Goodrich Lightfoot and Susannah his wife.

Pages 98-103. 16-17 Jan. 1749 [1750]. Philip Clayton and Ann his wife of St. Mark's Parish, Culpeper County, to John Parks of same. Lease and release; for £17.17.3. 230 acres, part of a deed granted to Philip Clayton from the Proprietor's Office 25 June 1748 ... John Rennolds's line ... another tract of said Clayton's ... line of John Spotswood's Esqr. ... corner of a tract formerly granted by patent to Francis Kirtley ... corner to said Parks and John Faver ...
                                  P. Clayton
                                 Ann Clayton
    Wit: Richard Thomas, Eliza. Thomas, John Faver.
    18 Jan. 1749 [1750]. Acknowledged by Philip Clayton Gent. and Ann his wife.

Pages 103-07. 16-17 Jan. 1749 [1750]. Philip Clayton and Ann his wife of St. Mark's Parish, Culpeper County, to John Faver of same. Lease and release; for £9.17.3 current money. 70 acres, part of a deed granted to Philip Clayton from the Proprietor's Office 25 June 1748 ... corner to John Parks and said Faver's tracts whereon they now live ... corner to Faver and Robert Slaughter Gent. ... corner to Thomas Covington, Alexr. McQueen and John Rennolds ...
P. Clayton
Ann Clayton
  Wit: Richard Thomas, Eliza. Thomas, John Parks.
   18 Jan. 1749 [1750]. Acknowledged by Philip Clayton Gent. and Ann his wife.

Pages 108-09. 16 Nov. 1749. John Bond of Culpeper County, planter, to Thomas Parks Junr. For natural love and affection which John Bond hath to Mary his now wife and to his daughter Elizabeth the wife of Bloomfield Long the Younger and to his daughter Mary the wife of Benjamin Long and to the intent of advancing his family. Negro slaves Hannah and her child Phillis and all other slaves that John Bond shall hereafter be possessed of.
   John Bond and Mary his wife and the survivor of them to enjoy the possession of the slaves and their increase during their lives, and after their decease the slaves to be equally divided, one half to Elizabeth Long during her natural life and after her decease to the children of Elizabeth Long equally, and the other half to Mary Long during her natural life and after her decease to the children of Mary Long equally.
John (J) Bond
  Wit: Roger Dixon, Jno. Bramham Junr., Henry Field Junr.
   18 Jan. 1749 [1750]. Proved by Roger Dixon, John Bramham Junr. and Henry Field Junr.

Pages 109-10. 18 Jan. 1749 [1750]. Robert Freeman of Culpeper County to Nathan Nalle of same. Lease for the life of Freeman. 100 acres in the little fork of Rappahannock River above the said Freeman's mill run including the plantation whereon Nathan now lives. Annual rent, 530 pounds of tobacco.
Robert (R) Freeman
  Wit: Samuel Parks, Christopher (C) Huckins, Thomas Dillard Junr.
   18 Jan. 1749 [1750]. Proved by Samuel Parks and Christopher Hutchins.
   15 Feb. 1749 [1750]. Proved by Thomas Dillard Junr.

Pages 111-12. 18 Jan. 1749 [1750]. Robert Freeman of Culpeper County to Christopher Hutchins of same. Lease for the life of Freeman. 100 acres in the little fork Rappahannock River ... at the mouth of my mill run ... to the mouth of a small run that runneth into the midd dam of the south side ... runing across to John Shakleford's line. Annual rent, 500 pounds of tobacco.
Robert (R) Freeman

Wit: Nathan Nall, Samuel Parks, ThomasDillard Junr.
18 Jan. 1749 [1750]. Proved by Nathan Nall and Samuel Parks.
13 Feb. 1749 [1750]. Proved by Thomas Dillard Junr.

Pages 112-15. 25 Nov. 1748. Matthew Stanton and Mary his wife
of Orange County to William Beverley of Essex County, Gent.
For 2988½ pounds of tobacco. Mortgage to secure 996 pounds
of tobacco to be paid 30 June next ensuing and 996 pounds of
tobacco upon 30 June 1750 and 996 pounds of tobacco on 30 June
1751.   The right of dower of Matthew and Mary his wife to 871
acres whereon they now dwell, being formerly her late husband
William Neal's ...   Also two feather beds and bed cloaths,
ten head of cattle marked with a swallow fork and slit in
each ear, one mare branded with a survell stirrup iron on, one
other mare branded on the buttock and sholder and a young horse
two years old, all on the said plantation.
                         Matt. Stanton
                         Mary (M) Stanton
    Wit: Thos. Chew, Frans: Moore, Rush Hudson, Thomas Finnell,
Jno. Bramham Junr.
    18 May 1749. Proved by Thomas Chew and John Bramham Junr.
    15 Feb. 1749 [1750]. Proved by Rush Hudson.
    22 July [1749]. Commission to Goodrich Lightfoot, Philip
Clayton, William Lynn and Ambrose Powell, Gent., to receive
the acknowledgment of Mary wife of Matthew Stanton to the
deed.
    19 Sept. 1749. Mary wife of Matthew Stanton is willing the
same should be recorded.   Gr. Lightfoot
                              Ambrose Powell

Pages 115-16. 15 Feb. 1749/50. [John Smith] to Robert Smith
of Culpeper County. For 10 shillings. All my joiners and
carpenters tools together with a chest and what books I have,
also a gun, a saddle and bridle, as likewise all my wearing
apparrel after my death.
                         John Smith
    Wit: Robert Williams, William Pound, Robert Williams Junr.
    I constitute Robert Williams my attorney to acknowledge
the deed.
                         John Smith
    15 Feb. 1749 [1750]. Proved by Robert Williams, William
Pound and Robert Williams Junr.

Pages 116-18. 6 Nov. 1749. Samuel Hildrup of the Town of
Fredericksburg and Elizabeth his wife to Adam Stephen of same,
Doctor of Physic. For £60 current money.   Moiety of 1482
acres, or 741 acres. By pattent 8 March 1733 there was
granted unto Mary and Elizabeth Taliaferro 1482 acres in St.
Mark's Parish, in the first fork of the Rappadan River.
Elizabeth Taliaferro hath since intermarried with Samuel
Hildrup.   Samll. Hildrup
                         Eliza (/) Hildrup
    Wit: Chas. Dick, Fielding Lewis, Roger Dixon.
    15 March 1749 [1750]. Acknowledged by Samuel Hildrup.
    6 Nov. 1749. Commission to Fielding Lewis, Charles Dick and

William Lynn, Gent., to receive the acknowledgment of Elizabeth wife of Samuel Hildrup.

7 Nov. 1749. Elizabeth Hildrup is willing that the deed should be recorded.   Fielding Lewis
Chas. Dick

Pages 119-21. 13 March 1749/50. William Rucker of St. Thomas' Parish, Culpeper County, planter, to William Twyman of same. For £40 current money. 123 acres ... corner to Thomas Cofer ... Philip Stockdale's corner ... above the fork ... courses of the run to a fork of a branch that falleth into the run ...
Wm. Rucker
Honour (X) Rucker
Wit: Robt. Sharman, Benja. Powell, Richd. Vawter.

15 March 1749. Acknowledged by William Rucker. Honour the wife of William relinquished her right of dower.

Pages 121-26. 7-8 Feb. 1750. John Vawter of Essex County to Ephraim Rucker and Margaret his wife of Culpeper County. Lease and release; for the love and good will he hath to his son-in-law and daughter Ephraim and Margaret Rucker and for 5 shillings. 200 acres, part of a tract granted John Vawter for 700 acres by patent 20 July 1736 ... corner to Kirtley and Stanton ...
Jno. Vawter
Wit: Bartholomew Vawter, Richard Vawter Senr. [Junr. in release], Angus Vawter, Augustine Vawter, Richd. Vawter.

15 March 1749 [1750]. Proved by Richard Vawter, Richard Vawter Junr., and Angus Vawter.

Pages 126-31. 7-8 Feb. 1750. John Vawter of Essex County to Angus Vawter of same. Lease and release; for the love and good will that he hath for his son [in release] Angus Vawter and for 5 shillings. 250 acres, being one half of a tract granted to John Vawter for 700 acres by pattent 20 July 1736 (except 200 acres which John Vawter hath already given to Ephraim Rucker and Margaret his wife) ... corner to Kirtley ... to Conway's land ... line that divides this land from the other half which is allotted for Richard Vawter son of the aforesaid John Vawter ...
Jno. Vawter
Wit: Bartholomew Vawter, Richard Vawter jr., Augustine Vawter, Richd. Vawter.

15 March 1749 [1750]. Proved by Richard Vawter, Richard Vawter jr., and Augustine Vawter.

Pages 131-36. 7-8 Feb. 1750. John Vawter of Essex County to Richard Vawter of Orange County. Lease and release; for the love and good will he hath for his son Richard Vawter and 5 shillings. 250 acres being one half of a tract granted unto John Vawter for 700 acres by pattent 20 July 1736 (except 200 acres which John Vawter hath already given and sold to Ephraim Rucker and Margaret his wife) ... to Conway's line ... line which divides this land from the other divident which is allotted for Angus Vawter son of the aforesaid John Vawter ...

to Kirtley's land ... to Ephraim and Margaret Rucker's land ...
Jno. Vawter
Wit: Bartholomew Vawter, Richard Vawter junr., Angus Vawter, Augustine Vawter.
15 March 1749 [1750]. Proved by Richard Vawter Junr., Angus Vawter and Augustine Vawter.

Pages 137-39. 12 March 1749 [1750]. Frances Thornton of St. George's Parish, Spotsylvania County, widow of Francis Thornton Gent., late of said parish, to John Frogg of Hamilton Parish, Prince William County, and Michael Wallace of Brunswick Parish, King George County. For 5 shillings. All interest she may claim in 1400 acres during her life.
Francis Thornton and Frances his wife for £30 current money by deeds of lease and release 3 March 1746 did sell unto John Frogg and Michael Wallace two tracts in Orange County, now in Culpeper County, containing 1400 acres, by deeds remaining in the Clerk's Office. Frances has never been privately examined as the law requires to prevent disputes with relation to her right of dower.
Frances Thornton
Wit: Robt. Shedden, Roger Dixon, William Strother.
13 March 1749 [1750]. Proved by Roger Dixon and William Strother.
16 March 1749 [1750]. Proved by Robert Shedden.

Pages 139-40. 15 March 1749 [1750]. John Shakleford of Culpeper County to Richard Nalle of same. Lease of 100 acres in the little Fork of Rappahannock River ... upon Indian Run near a path ... hickory on a hill side ...   For 21 years; if Shakleford shall live longer then the lease shall continue to the end of Shakleford's life. Yearly rent, 500 pounds of tobacco after 10 May 1752. Nalle shall not keep more than four tithables besides himself in constant working on the land.
John Shakleford
Richard Nalle
16 March 1749 [1750]. Acknowledged by John Shakleford and Richard Nalle.

Pages 140-47. 15-15 March 1749 [1750]. Thomas Dillard of Culpeper County, planter, and Winifred his wife to Humphrey Wallis of Fredericksburg in Spotsylvania County, merchant. Lease and release; for £100 current money.   1100 acres granted to Thomas Dillard by the Right Honorable Thomas Lord Fairfax, Proprietor of the Northern Neck, 24 Nov. 1749 ... on the north side of Muddy Run corner to land granted by patent to John Latham, now George Dillard's ... head of a pond ... near Capt. Eastham's line ... corner to the said Robert Eastham ... on a small fork of Cabbin Branch ... line of William Tapp's ... line of Lewis Davis Yancey's land ... Thomas and James Graves's line ... side of a hill near Cabbin Branch ... line of the land purchased by Philemon Kavanaugh deceased.
Thoms: Dillard
Winifred (X) Dillard

Wit: William Strother, Fras. Slaughter Junr., Robert Coleman.
16 March 1749 [1750]. Acknowledged by Thomas Dillard and Winifred his wife.

Pages 147-51. 6-7 Nov. 1749. Robert Hutchison of St. Mark's Parish, Culpeper County, to John Stone Syffer of same. Lease and release; for £60 current money. 200 acres ... corner to John Sutton ... near Jacob Manspoile's line ...
                              Robert Hutchison
   Wit: Zach: Blankinbecker, Johanness Huffman [? signed in German], Matthias (X) Roush.
   19 April 1850. Acknowledged by Robt. Hutchison.

Pages 151-53. 20 April 1750. Joseph Thomas and Sarah his wife of Orange County to Calem Price of Culpeper County. For 3500 pounds of tobacco. 150 acres on the south branch of the Gourd Vine River ... at the mouth of Long Branch ... to Thomas' back line ... crossing the end of a mountain called the Giant's Castle to a corner on the river above the mountain ... including the plantation setled by Thomas Hannon on the north side of the river.
                              Joseph Thomas
   Received by the hands of Robert Eastham 3500 pounds of tobacco.
                              Joseph Thomas
   20 April 1750. Acknowledged by Joseph Thomas.

Pages 154-56. 17-18 April 1750. James Barnett of St. Mark's Parish, Culpeper County, carpenter, to Spencer Bobo of same, planter. Lease and release; for £10 current money. 100 acres on the branches of Rappadan and Robinson rivers ... near the ridge between the Rappadan and Robinson rivers corner to John Medley ... [release also describes the land as on the branches of the Rappadan and Robinson rivers near the Lost Mountains].
                              James Barnett
   Wit: David Davis, Spencer (X) Bobo, Junr.
   17 May 1750. Acknowledged by James Barnett.

Pages 156-58. 17 May 1750. William Hensley of St. Thomas' Parish, Orange County, planter, to Jacob Ward of abovesaid parish, Culpeper County, planter. For £25 current money. 200 acres part of a patent granted to Thomas Zachary and James Finnie for 400 acres in St. Thomas' Parish in the Little fork on the branches of the Rappadan River ... south east side of the road that goes from Crawford's ...
                              William (X) Hensley
                              Jane (X) Hensley
   Wit: James Rucker, Spencer Bobo, James Barnett.
   17 May 1750. Acknowledged by William Hensley and Jane his wife.

Pages 159-61. 17 May 1750. Henry Downs Junr. of St. Thomas' Parish, Orange County, Thomas Jackson of same, planter, to William Rucker of St. Thomas' Parish, Culpeper County. For

£95 current money.   100 acres ... on the Rappadan River ... on
a hill by David Jackson's fence ... on a branch ...   Also one
grist mill standing on Rapadan River and adjoining to the
abovesaid land.   Henry Downs
                                        Thomas (T) Jackson
    Wit: Richard Thomas, Thos. Jones.
    17 May 1750. Acknowledged by Henry Downs and Thomas Jackson.
Jane, the wife of Henry, relinquished her right of dower.

Pages 161-63. 11 March 1749 [1750]. William Cridinton of St.
Mary's Parish, Louisa County, joyner, to Nathaniel Dickerson
of St. Margaret's Parish, Spotsylvania County. For £15 current
money.   100 acres ... on Beautiful Run ...
                                   William Crittenden
    Wit: Thomas Jones, Richard Thomas.
    17 May 1750. Acknowledged by William Crittenden. Eleanor,
the wife of William, relinquished her right of dower.

Pages 163-65. 9 May 1750. Thomas Jackson of St. Thomas'
Parish, Orange County, planter, to Isaac Jackson of St. Thomas'
Parish, Culpeper County, planter. For £5 current money.   100
acres ... corner to Isaac Smith ... corner to David Jackson ...
by the road ... William Rucker's corner ... head of a branch ...
to the river ...
                                   Thomas (T) Jackson
    17 May 1750. Acknowledged by Thomas Jackson.

Pages 165-67. 11 May 1750. Thomas Jackson of St. Thomas'
Parish, Orange County, planter, to David Jackson of St. Thomas'
Parish, Culpeper County, planter. For £5 current money.   100
acres ... corner to Isaac Smith and Isaac Jackson ... down the
branch ... corner to James Zachary ... to another branch ...
                                   Thomas (T) Jackson
    17 May 1750. Acknowledged by Thomas Jackson.

Pages 167-69. 11 May 1750. Thomas Jackson of St. Thomas'
Parish, Orange County, planter, to William Rucker of St. Thomas'
Parish, Culpeper County. For £5 current money.   100 acres ...
corner to William Rucker ... up the branch ... on the road ...
                                   Thomas (T) Jackson
    17 May 1750. Acknowledged by Thomas Jackson.

Pages 169-71. 17 May 1750. Tully Choice of Orange County and
Anne his wife to Matthew Tool of Culpeper County. For £95.6.-
current money.   100 acres in St. Mark's Parish in the fork of
Rappahannock River ... which was conveyed to Matthew Tool and
Elizabeth his wife by William Duff 10 April 1740 and to the
heirs of her body begotten in lawfull wedlock, and by Matthew
Tool and Elizabeth his wife was conveyed to Tully Choice 7 Aug.
1743.   Tully Choice
                                   Anne Choice
    Wit: Joseph Thomas, James Rucker, Beaumount Sutton.
    17 May 1750. Acknowledged by Tully Choice and Anne his wife.

Pages 171-73. 8 May 1750. Francis Kirtley of St. Thomas'

Parish, Culpeper County, to James Rucker of same. Lease for 99 years of 150 acres whereon James Rucker now lives ... at the mouth of Garth's Run ... to Francis Kirtley's line ... to Farrow's Run ... up the river ... within the said bounds of a parcel of black walnut trees standing at the lower end of the cornfield not to be sell, destroied nor made use of. If James Rucker should want any of them to saw into plank, liberty is given to James Rucker but not to his assigns. Rent, 100 pounds of tobacco to be added to the 900 pounds of tobacco for each tithable above two that James Rucker takes in to make a crop.

Francis (X) Kirtley
Wit: Martin (X) Dewitt, Charles (N) Neal, William Henderson.
17 May 1750. Acknowledged by Francis Kirtley.

Pages 173-74. 9 Dec. 1749. Adam Stephen of the town of Fredericksburg, practitioner in physick, to Samuel Hildrup of the town of Fredericksburg. For £60 current money. 741 acres in the first fork of the Rappadan River, being the moiety or half part of 1482 acres granted by patent 8 March 1733 to Mary and Elizabeth Taliaferro ... being the same land which Samuel Hildrup and Elizabeth his wife sold to Adam Stephen 6 Nov. 1749 ...

Adam Stephen
Wit: W. Russell, Frans. Strother Junr., Francis (X) Strother.
15 March 1749 [1750]. Proved by Francis Strother.
16 March 1749 [1750]. Proved by William Russell.
17 May 1750. Proved by Francis Strother Junr.

Pages 175-77. 17 May 1750. John Smith of Culpeper County, planter, to Abraham Cooper of same, carpenter. For £25 current money. Tract on the north side of the North Branch of the Gourd Vine River, part of 430 acres taken up by Francis Browning, the lower part of which 430 acres Browning gave to his son Nicholas Browning and the upper part Francis Browning sold to Thomas Washbourn and Wasbourn conveyed to John Smith ... corner to John Smith and Nicholas Browning ... up the meanders of the river ...

John (J S) Smith
17 May 1750. Acknowledged by John Smith.

Pages 177-78. 14 March 1749/50. Thomas Stanton of Culpeper County, planter, to William Pearson of same, planter. Lease from 5 Nov. 1747 for 21 years of tract joining on the tenement where Michael Pearson now dwells ... on Stanton River, being a corner of Michael Pearson's line ... down the river ... to lick branch ... to the Cabbin Branch ... Yearly rent, 450 pounds of tobacco, the first four years to be rent free.

Thos. Stanton
Wit: Jeremiah Earley, Michael (X) Peirson, Abraham (A) Eddins.
17 May 1750. Acknowledged by Thomas Stanton.

Pages 178-80. 17-17 May 1750. Robert Froggit of St. Mark's Parish, Culpeper County, to Samuel Cage of same. Duplicate agreement, one signed by each. Samuel Cage doth bind himself an apprentice unto Robert Froggit to learn the trade of a blacksmith for three years.

Saml. (X) Cage
Robert (R F) Froggit

17 May 1750. Acknowledged by Samuel Cage and Robert Froggit.

Pages 180-83. 20-21 June 1750. Philip Clayton and Ann his wife of Culpeper County to William Cowne, merchant, of King William County. Lease and release; for £80 current money. 600 acres granted to Philip Clayton by the Right Honourable Thomas, Lord Fairfax, 25 June 1748 ... corner to John Durret ... hiccory on Muddy Run Mountain ... line of Messrs. Bryan and William Henry Fairfax ... head of a branch in the line of a patent granted to Colo. Henry Willis ... Walter Butler's line ...

P. Clayton
Ann Clayton

21 June 1750. Acknowledged by Philip Clayton and Ann his wife.

Pages 184-86. 21 June 1750. Goodrich Lightfoot and Susannah Lightfoot his wife of Culpeper County to Jacob Kendrick of Caroline County. For 20 current money. £240 acres ... on the north side of Potato Run ... corner to William Kelly ... up the run ... corner to Leonard Zeiglar ... crossing the run ... corner to Frederick Cassler ... corner to William Watts near his plantation ... granted to Goodrich Lightfoot 29 June 1749...

Gr. Lightfoot
Susanna Lightfoot

21 June 1752. Acknowledged by Goodrich Lightfoot and Susannah his wife.

Pages 186-87. 21 June 1750. Thomas Stanton of Culpeper County, planter, to John Simpson of same, planter. Lease for 21 years from 5 Nov. 1747 of land joyning on the lower side of the plantation whereon Thomas Stanton now lives ... at Rock Hall on the north side of Stanton River ... Thomas Stanton's patent line to the river ... Thomas Stanton's fence ... Thomas Stanton's lower path where it now goes to the road ... dividing line between Thomas Stanton and Kirtley ... Yearly rent after the first year rent free, 450 pounds of tobacco upon the feast of the Nativity of Our Blessed Lord Christ.

Stanton doth agree to find timber for rails and firewood on his land for the use of the tenement when all timber is used on the tenement.

Thos. Stanton
John Simpson

Wit: B. Roberts, G. Hume.

21 June 1750. Acknowledged by Thomas Stanton and John Simpson.

Pages 188-90. 14 Nov. 1749. William Beverley of Blandfield, Essex County, Esqr., to John Gett of Culpeper County, planter. Lease of 100 acres, part of Elkwood ... corner to another lott of the said Gett's ... For lives of John Gett and Stephen his son and James Jett his son and the longest liver. Yearly rent, 474 pounds of tobacco on 27 November.

If Gett shall work more than two tithables besides himself, to pay for every tithable beside the two and himself 105 pounds of tobacco additional rent. John Gett shall keep an orchard of one hundred good apple trees in good repair well fenced safe from cattle, horses, goats and sheep and will keep all houses in good repair.

W. Beverley

Wit: W. Russell, Gabriel Jones, Joseph Amiss.
16 March 1749 [1750]. Proved by William Russell.
19 April 1750. Proved by Joseph Amiss.
19 July 1750. Proved by Gabriel Jones.

Pages 190-92. 14 Nov. 1749. William Beverley of Blandfield, Essex County, Esqr., to William Crawford of Culpeper County, planter. Lease of 107 acres, part of Elkwood ... on the bank of Hedgman River ... saving liberty of making a path thro the land where it shall be necessary. For lives of his three sons John Crawford, William Crawford and Reuben Crawford and the longest liver. Yearly rent 474 pounds of tobacco on 27 November. If Crawford shall work more than two tithables besides himself to pay for every tithable beside the two and himself 105 pounds of tobacco additional rent.

William Crawford shall keep an orchard of one hundred good apple trees in good repair, well fenced, safe from cattle, horses, goats and sheep and will keep all houses in good repair.

W. Beverley

Wit: W. Russell, Gabriel Jones, John Gett.
15 March 1749 [1750]. Proved by John Gett.
16 March 1749 [1750]. Proved by William Russell.
19 July 1750. Proved by Gabriel Jones.

Pages 192-94. 13 Nov. 1749. William Beverley of Blandfield, Essex County, Esqr., to William Abbet of Culpeper County, planter. Lease of 104 acres, part of Elkwood ... on a branch ... line of Waddington Abbett lott ... saving liberty of making a path thro the land where it shall be necessary. For lives of William Abbet, Elizabeth his wife and Roger their son and the longest liver. Yearly rent 474 pounds of tobacco on 27 November. If Abbet shall work more than two tithables besides himself to pay for every tithable beside the two and himself 105 pounds of tobacco additional rent.

William Abbet shall keep an orchard of one hundred good apple trees in good repair, well fenced, safe from cattle, horses, goats and sheep and will keep all houses in good repair.

W. Beverley

Wit: W. Russell, Gabriel Jones, Waddington (W) Abbet.
19 July 1750. Proved by William Russell, Gabriel Jones and Waddington Abbet.

Pages 195-97. 13 Nov. 1749. William Beverley of Blandfield, Essex County, Esqr., to Waddington Abbet of Culpeper, planter. Lease of 104 acres, part of Elkwood ... in a glade ... William Beverley's out line ... For lives of Waddington Abbet, his sons William and Waddington and the longest liver. Yearly rent 474 pounds of tobacco on 27 November. If Abbet shall work more than two tithables besides himself to pay for every tithable beside the two and himself 105 pounds of tobacco additional rent.

Waddington Abbet shall keep an orchard of one hundred good apple trees in good repair, well fenced, safe from cattle, horses, goats and sheep and will keep all houses in good repair
W. Beverley
Wit: W. Russell, Gabriel Jones, William (W) Abbet.
19 July 1750. Proved by William Russell, Gabriel Jones and William Abbet.

Pages 197-99. 19 July 1750. Christopher Houchin and Elizabeth his wife of Culpeper County to Samuel Parks of same. For £30 current money.   147 acres above Muddy Run and adjoining the land whereon Parks now dwells ... branch in Kavanaugh's line ... corner of William Kelly ... down the branch...
Christopher (C) Houchins
Eliza. Hutchings
19 July 1750. Acknowledged by Christopher Hutchings and Elizabeth his wife.

Pages 200-01. 3 Jan. 1749 [1750]. John Wynill Sanders of Culpeper County to Robert Coleman of same. For £36.2.6 current money.   Two Negroes Mingo and Phillis.

For 5 shillings mortgage of Negro boy Harry, if John Wynill Sanders should not have a good title to Mingo and Phillis.
John Wynill Sanders
Wit: P. Clayton, Wm. Brown, B. Fargeson.
20 July 1750. Proved by Philip Clayton and William Brown.

Pages 202-03. 16 Aug. 1750. Matthias Smith of St. Mark's Parish, Culpeper County, to Nicholas Smith of same. For natural love and affection to Nicholas Smith his son.   100 acres in the first fork of Rappidan, part of a tract granted to Matthias Smith and Matthias Barler by patent 24 June 1726.
Matthias Smith [in German]
Wit: Roger Dixon, Richard Thomas, R. Slaughter.
16 Aug. 1750. Acknowledged by Matthias Smith.

Pages 203-07. 16-16 Aug. 1750. George Long of St. Mark's Parish, Culpeper County, to Michael Russell of same. Lease and release; for £10 current money.   105 acres ... at the mouth of a small branch above Long's Foard to the line of George Long ... corner of Matthias Castler ... by the Robinson River ...
Georg Long
16 Aug. 1750. Acknowledged by George Long.

Pages 207-13. 2-3 Aug. 1750. Joseph Dewett of Culpeper County to Andrew Rosse and Alexander and Daniel Campbell of King George County. Lease and release; for £185 current money. 880 acres ... line of Collo. Carter's Barrow low ground tract ... by a branch ... in Carter's line where Chissam's line intersects ... corner to Crim and Detheridge ... Fishback's line ... dividing line between Dewett and Green ...

18

Joseph Dewett
    Wit: G. Hume, Thos. Slaughter, Chs. Strother, Fredk. (F) Fishback.
    16 Aug. 1750. Proved by George Hume, Thomas Slaughter, Charles Strother and Frederick Fishback.

Pages 213-17. 4-5 April 1750. William Nash of Culpeper County to John Asher of same. Lease and release; for £37 current money. 200 acres ... in Collo. John Spotswood's line and corner to a patent granted to James Horsnell (the said 200 acres being part of the said patent) ... Francis Micall's line ...
                            W. Nash
    Wit: James Pollard, G. Hume, G. Hume Junr.
    Receipt. Wit: G. Hume, John Wetheral.
    16 Aug. 1750. Acknowledged by William Nash. Betty, the wife of William, relinquished her right of dower.

Pages 217-19. 18 Oct. 1750. Robert Coleman of St. Mark's Parish, Culpeper County, and Sarah his wife, to William Goggan of Lunenburgh Parish, Richmond County. For £25 current money. 300 acres in St. Thomas' Parish, Culpeper County, which was patented by Robert Coleman and bought of Coleman by Daniel Brown and is part of a patent granted to Coleman 28 Sept. 1732 ... bounded by the lines of Joseph Abell (who holds 100 acres out of the patent) and the land formerly held by Daniel Brown now by Rowland Cornelious and the Revd. Mr. John Thompson's land which he bought of Samuel Farguson, according to the bounds of the patent not before conveyed to Abell ...
                            Robert Coleman
                            Sarah Coleman
    18 Oct. 1750. Acknowledged by Robert Coleman and Sarah his wife.

Pages 220-21. 1750. Richard Mauldin of Caroline County to Spencer Bobo of Culpeper County. For £50 current money. 50 acres, part of a pattent granted to Richard Mauldin 1736 ... corner of William Sparks ... on Dark run corner to Benjamin Powell ... to the mouth of White Oak Run ...
                            R. Mauldin
    Wit: Thos. Sparks, William (X) Sparks, Benja. Powell.
    18 Oct. 1750. Proved by Thomas Sparks, William Sparks and Benjamin Powell.

Pages 221-23. 18 Oct. 1750. Ambross Powell of Culpeper County to Benjamin Powell of same. For 25 shillings. 25 acres in Parish of St. Mark, part of a deed granted to Ambrose Powell from the Proprietor's Office 27 June 1748 ... on Dark Run corner to Benjamin Powell ... crossing Dark Run twice ...
                            Ambrose Powell
    18 Oct. 1750. Acknowledged by Ambrose Powell, Gent.

Pages 227-29. 13 Aug. 1750. John Zachary of St. Thomas' Parish, Culpeper County, planter, to Thomas Watts of same. For £20 current money. 183 acres, part of a patent granted to Thomas Watts and John Zachary containing 333 acres, 7 July

1735 ... on Bland Ballard's line, James Barbour's line and Dixon's line ... Ann Zachary wife to John Zachary relinquishes all my right of dower.

John (X) Zachary

Wit: Benjamin Watts, Valentine Johnson, Ed. Watts.

18 Oct. 1750. Acknowledged by John Zachary. Ann the wife of John relinquished her right of dower.

Pages 229-30. 15 Nov. 1750. Michael Glore and Barbara his wife of St. Mark's Parish, Culpeper County, to George Glore, son of Michael and Barbara, of same. For natural love and affection. 300 acres in St. Mark's Parish on the north side of the Robinson River, being part of a tract of land out of a patent granted to George Moyer 28 Sept. 1728 ... north side of Robinson River ...

Michael (H) Glore

Wit: William Henderson, Tomitz Burs [Bow?], Michael (T) Holt Junr.

15 Nov. 1750. Acknowledged by Michael Glore.

Pages 231-33. 9 Nov. 1750. Martin Dewitt of St. Thomas' Parish, Culpeper County, to John Simpson of same. For £4 current money. 3 acres, part of that tract that Martin Dewitt had of Charles Neele in St. Thomas' Parish in the little fork on the north branch of the Rappadan River ... at Henry Downs Junr. upper corner on the river bank, thence up the Rappadan River to the mouth of a branch below Martin Dewitt's plantation called the Dogwood Branch ... John Simpson's line ...

Martin (X) Dewitt

Wit: William Henderson, Matthew Stanton, Charles (N) Neel.

15 Nov. 1750. Acknowledged by Martin Dewitt.

Pages 233-35. 15 Nov. 17[ ]. Edward Watts and Elizabeth his wife of Culpeper County to John Watts of same. For £42 current money. 180 acres ... corner to Henry Downs ... on a ridge of Neall Mountain ... in George Eastham's line ... to Thomas Rucker's line ... to David Tinsley's line ... to Henry Downs' line ...

Ed. Watts

Elizabeth Watts

Wit: Richard Thomas, Thomas Scott.

15 Nov. 1750. Acknowledged by Edward Watts and Elizabeth his wife.

Pages 235-38. 14-15 Nov. 1750. James Cotten and Sarah his wife of Culpeper County to James Johnson of same. Lease and release; for £15 current money. 100 acres ... corner to said Johnson on Buttock Run ... near the Reverend Mr. Thompson's fence ... to the south fork of the Gourd Vine River ... to John Brown's upper corner on the river ... part of a patent granted to Joseph Bloodworth and Conrade Amburger 2 Aug. 1736.

James (X) Cotten

Sarah (X) Cotten

15 Nov. 1750. Acknowledged by James Cotten and Sarah his wife.

Pages 238-40. 15 Nov. 1750. John Smith of Culpeper County
to John Cooper of same. For 300 acres on the south side of
the North fork of Gourd Vine River ... on the Upper Turnep
Branch in the back line of said Cooper's land ... on the river
... to John Cooper's lower corner ... part of a tract granted
to John Cooper by the Honorable Thomas, Lord Fairfax, for 400
acres 23 Aug. 1749.   130 acres on the north side of the
North River of Gourd Vine ... at John Smith's upper corner
from the river in Mr. William Duncan's line ... dividing line
between John Smith and Abraham Cooper ... being the upper part
of a tract formerly granted to Francis Browning for 430 acres
as by Browning's deed 4 Feb. 1747 will appear ...
John (J) Smith
15 Nov. 1750. Acknowledged by John Smith.

Pages 240-43. 15 Nov. 1750. John Cooper and Judith his wife
of Culpeper County to John Smith of same. For 150 acres on the
north side of the north fork of Guord Vine River ... at John
Smith's upper corner in Mr. William Duncan's line ... down the
meanders of the river to the dividing line between John Smith
and Abraham Cooper ... being the upper part of a tract formerly
granted to Francis Browning for 430 acres 4 Feb. 1747.   300
acres on the south side of the north fork of the Guord Vine
River ... on the Upper Turnip Branch in the back line of Cooper's
land ... down the meanders of the river to Cooper's lower
corner ... part of a tract granted to John Cooper for 400 acres
23 Aug. 1749.   John (J) Cooper
Judith Cooper
15 Nov. 1750. Acknowledged by John Cooper.

Pages 243-47. 15 Nov. 1750. John Spotswood of Spotsylvania
County, Esqr., son, heir and devisee of Alexander Spotswood
late of Orange County, Esqr., and Mary his wife, Elliott Benger
Gent., one of the executors of the last will and testament of
Alexander Spotswood, to Philip Rootes of King and Queen County,
Gent. For £141 current money.   470 acres in St. Mark's
Parish ... on the south side of a branch near the Courthouse
Road corner to the Revd. Mr. John Thompson ... in William Nash's
line ... to the main road ... up the road to Mr. Robert
Spotswood's line ... to Daniel Brown's corner ...
    Alexander Spotswood by his last will and testament 19 April
1740 did devise all his lands in Virginia to his eldest son
John Spotswood and to the heirs male of his body and for
default he gave the same to his son Robert, and annexed to the
lands and to descend therewith to his sons and their issue
male he bequeathed all his working slaves and their increase
which should be imployed in labour upon any of his lands at
the time of his decease, and gave unto his executors during the
minority of either of his sons power to lease any of his lands
(except his mine tract) and did bequeath to his son Robert
£3000 sterling, to his daughter Anna Catherina £2000 sterling
and to his daughter Dorothea £2000 sterling to be paid at their
respective ages of twenty one years or days of marriage and to
be raised by mortgage or sale of any part of his lands (his
mine tract excepted), and the will appointed his wife Butler

Spotswood, Elliott Benger and Robert Rose, Clerk, executrix
and executors, and since the death of Alexander Spotswood his
daughter Anna Catherine hath intermarried with Bernard Moore
of the County of King William, Gent., and the other daughter
Dorothea hath also intermarried with Nathaniel West Dandridge
of the County of King William, Gent., whereby the fortunes
devised to Anna Catherina and Dorothea are become payable and
it being found by experience that the growing rents and
profits of the estate charged with the fortunes are not
sufficient to raise the same and the other purposes mentioned
in the will, and it being also thought more expedient to
sell part of the land than to mortgage the same ...

John Spotswood
Mary Spotswood
Elliott Benger

17 Nov. [1750]. Commission to Robert Jackson, William
Hunter, Fielding Lewis, Anthony Strother and Charles Dick of
Spotsylvania County, Gent., to receive the acknowledgment of
Mary, wife of John Spotswood to sale 15 Nov. 1750 of 470 acres
19 Jan. 1750 [1751]. Mary, wife of John Spotswood, did
acknowledge the same.   Rob. Jackson
Fielding Lewis
15 Nov. 1750. Acknowledged by John Spotswood and Elliott
Benger, Esqrs.

Pages 247-50. 15 Nov. 1750. John Spotswood, Esqr., son,
heir and devisee of Alexander Spotswood, late of Orange
County, Esqr., deceased, and Mary his wife, Elliott Benger
Esqr., one of the executors of the last will and testament
of Alexander Spotswood, to Robert Coleman of Culpeper County.
For £24.2.- current money.   247 acres in St. Mark's Parish
... on a branch corner to Daniel Brown ... north side of
Bloodworth's Road ... on a ridge ...
[Provisions of Alexander Spotswood's will, as above, pp.
243-47]   John Spotswood
Mary Spotswood
Elliott Benger
15 Nov. 1750. Acknowledged by John Spotswood and Elliott
Benger, Esqrs.
17 Nov. [1750]. Commission to Robert Jackson, William
Hunter, Fielding Lewis, Anthony Strother and Charles Dick
of Spotsylvania County, Gent., to receive the acknowledgment
of Mary, wife of John Spotswood, to sale 15 Nov. 1750 of 247
acres.
19 Jan. 1750 [1751]. Mary, wife of John Spotswood, Esqr.,
acknowledged the same.   Rob. Jackson
Fielding Lewis

Page 251. 26 Dec. 1750. Walter Fitzgerald of Culpeper
County, planter, to Mosley Battaley of Spotsylvania County,
Gent. For 5.1.7½; mortgage to secure £9.1.7½ to be paid
within three months.   One dark gray mare branded on the near
buttock [a heart] and on the near shoulder [a square], also
three cows now with calf, the one a brown cow with both ears
cropp'd, one brindled cow with both ears cropp'd, two slits

in each ear and a hole in the left ear, one pyed cow with a
crop in each ear, one pyed steer two years old marked with
two slits and a crop in each ear and a hole in the left, one
red heifer two years old with a crop and two slits in each
ear and a hole in the left ear, and two bull yearlings, a red
one and a brindled one, and one cow yearling red, all the
yearlings unmarked, one feather bed, rugg and blankett, and
a pair of sheets, two iron potts and pothooks, one pewter dish
and three plates, seventeen shoats about one year old, two
sows and tenn piggs.
                        Walter (X) Fitzgerald
   Wit: Jno. Battaley, Saml. Battaley.
   21 March 1750 [1751]. Proved by John Battaley.

Pages 252-54.   March 1750 [1751]. Edward Herndon of Spotsylvania County to Edward Herndon Junr. of same. For £50 current
money.   400 acres in the Little Fork of Rappahannock River ...
corner to a survey made for the heirs of Captain John Grant in
Captain Compton's line ... on a hill ... on the west side of
the Hedgman River ... by the mouth of a branch on Hedgman River
... on the falling ground of Jobbers Mountain ... line of
George Fairfax Esqr. ... to Captain Compton's line ...
                        Edwd. Herndon
   Wit: Joseph Wood, Jno. Battaley, Samuel Simpson, Abraham
Simpson.
   21 March 1750 [1751]. Proved by Joseph Wood, John
Battaley and Abraham Simpson.

Pages 254-56. 21 March 1750 [1751]. Ambrose Powell of Culpeper
County to Christian and Eberhart Ryner of same. For £35
current money.   530 acres in the Parish of Saint Mark being
the full contents of a deed granted to Ambrose Powell for
530 acres 27 June 1748 ... in Benjamin Powell's line ...
corner to Benjamin and Ambrose Powell ... near the head of a
branch ... corner to John Bruce ...
                        Ambrose Powell
   21 March 1750 [1751]. Acknowledged by Ambrose Powell.

Pages 256-60. 20-21 March 1750 [1751]. John Carpenter of
St. Mark's Parish, Culpeper County, planter, to Lawrence
Garr of same, weaver. Lease and release; for £30 current
money.   150 acres by patent 20 June 1733 in St. Mark's Parish
in the Little Fork of the Rappidan River ... in Michael Cook's
line ... corner to Cook on the Pass Run ... on a ridge corner
to Matthew Blancumbeker ... on the side of a mountain ...
                        John (X) Carpenter
   21 March 1750 [1751]. Acknowledged by John Carpenter.
Barbara the wife of John relinquished her right of dower.

Page 260. 13 Dec. 1750. I certifie that I do not intend
to stand to my husband Thomas Watts' will, neither do I intend
to take any advantage by it.
                        Esther Watts
   Wit: James Barbour, Benjamin Watts.
   21 March 1750 [1751]. Proved by James Barbour and Benjamin
Watts.

Pages 260-66. 23-24 Aug. 1750. Edward Dougharty and John Dougharty, both living in Lancaster Co., Pa., to Doctor William Lynn of Fredericksburg, Va. Lease and release; for £23.10.- current money. 400 acres in the fork of the Rappidan River ... corner to Thomas Walker ... corner to John Bruce ... being a patent granted to Edward Dougharty and John Dougharty 6 June 1735.   Edwd. Dougharty
                              John Dougharty
     Wit: James Hunter, Humphrey Wallis, Thomas Skinker, Gr. Lightfoot, Wm. Marye.
     20 Sept. 1750. Proved by William Marye.
     21 Sept. 1750. Proved by Goodrich Lightfoot.
     21 March 1750 [1751]. Proved by James Hunter.
     24 Aug. 1750. Bond of Edward Dougharty and John Dougharty of Lancaster Co., Pa., unto Doctor William Lynn of Fredericksburgh. For £47 current money. To perform the covenants mentioned in the indenture of lease and release for 400 acres.
                              Ed. Dougharty
                              John Dougharty
     Wit: James Hunter, Humphrey Wallis, Thomas Skinker, William Marye.
     20 Sept. 1750. Proved by William Marye
     21 March 1750 [1751]. Proved by James Hunter.

Pages 266-67. 19 March 1750 [1751]. Anthony Scott of Culpeper County to Thomas Corbin and my daughter Elizabeth Corbin wife of Thomas Corbin of same. For love, good will and affection.   105 acres in the little fork of Rappahannock River ... upon a branch between the plantation on the premises and the plantation whereon John Burk formerly lived on the south side of the branch opposite to the mouth of Chestnut Branch ... fork of the branch ... near the Peaked Mountain Road ...
                              Anthony Scott
     Wit: John (J) Cooper, James J W) Wilson, Thomas (T) Washbourn.
     21 March 1750 [1751]. Proved by John Cooper, James Wilson and Thomas Wasburn.

Pages 268-69. 20 June 1750. Micajah Poole of Culpeper County to William Hunter of Spotsylvania County. Mortgage to secure payment of £154.8.6 before 1 December next. Three Negroes named Bacchus, Diana and Juno, eight head of cattle, two horses, one mare, two feather beds, six chairs, and three iron potts.
                              Micajah Poole
     Wit: James Hunter, Charles Massey, Robt. Hill.
     21 March 1750 [1751]. Acknowledged by Micajah Poole.

Page 269. 5 Nov. 1750. Robert Loyns of Culpeper County to William Green of same. For 1000 pounds of tobacco. One young bay gelding branded on the near buttock thus 3, one saddle and housing, one feather bed and furniture, one hogshead of tobacco now under prize almost full, and all the tobacco which I now have hanging and in bulk.

Robert (R) Loyns
Wit: Henry Field junr., W. Ball, Jas. (J) Rains.
22 March 1750 [1751]. Proved by Henry Field Junr.

Pages 270-72. 18 April 1751. John Read and Winefred his wife of Culpeper County to William Lightfoot of Richmond County. For £69.17.6 current money. 100 acres, corner to Mr. Robert Green and Isaac Norman's land ... in the low grounds of Flat Run ... line of a patent granted to Norman ... part of a tract granted to Norman for 420 acres 30 June 1726 and sold by Norman to Read.   John Read
Winifred (M) Read
Wit: Francis Slaughter, Francis Slaughter Junr., R. Slaughter.
11 April 1751. Acknowledged by John Read and Winifred his wife.

Pages 272-74. 3 Jan. 1750 [1751]. George Thompson of Saint Thomas' Parish, Culpeper County, to Seth Thurston of same. For £34 current money. 100 acres in St. Thomas' Parish in the little fork on the branches of the Rappidan River being the same parcel of land that George Thompson purchased of William Pellam ... on Maple Run ...
George (X) Thompson
Catherine (C) Thompson
Wit: William Henderson, John Buford, Charles Walker.
18 April 1751. Acknowledged by George Thompson.

Pages 274-75. 30 March 1751. Henry Downs of Orange County to Seth Thurston of Culpeper County. For £10 sterling. 100 acres joyning to the land where Seth Thurston now lives and being all the land that belongs to Henry Downs between Rocky Run and Maple Run ...
Hen: Downs
Wit: Richard Quinn, Darby (D) Quinn, Charles Walker.
18 April 1751. Proved by Richard Quinn, Darby Quinn and Charles Walker.

Pages 275-77. 1751. Charles Walker of Culpeper County to Seth Thurston of same. For £10 current money. 50 acres ... in Downs' line ... to Walker's and Thurston's corner ... on the north side of the Cattail Branch ...
Charles Walker
Wit: Richard Quinn, George Bruce.
18 April 1751. Acknowledged by Charles Walker.

Pages 277-78. 1 April 1751. Henry Downs of Orange County to Charles Walker of Culpeper County. For £10 sterling. 100 acres ... at Seth Thurston's corner ... to Henry Downs' line ... to the Cattail Branch ... mouth of the branch in Maple Run ...
Hen: Downs
Wit: Richard Quinn, Darby (D) Quinn, Seth Thurston.
18 April 1751. Proved by Richard Quinn, Darby Quinn and Seth Thurston.

Pages 279-80. 18 April 1751. Seth Thurston of Culpeper County to Charles Walker of same. For £10 current money. 50 acres ... at Thurston's and Finney's corner ... to Downs' line ...
                          Seth Thurston
   Wit: Richard Quinn, George Bruce.
   18 April 1751. Acknowledged by Seth Thurston.

Pages 280-82. 18 April 1751. Thomas Brown and Elianor his wife of Culpeper County to Robert Coleman of same. For £300 current money. 400 acres ... being part in the said county and part in Augusta County ... on the south side of the Blue Ridge of Mountains ... crossing some branches of Thornton's River ... on the north side of the Blue Ridge ...
                          Thomas Brown
                          Elianor Brown
   Wit: Henry Field Junr., Chas. Kavanaugh, Fras. Slaughter Junr.
   18 April 1751. Acknowledged by Thomas Brown and Elianor his wife.

Pages 282-84. 16 May 1751. James Pendleton and Elizabeth his wife of Culpeper County to John Barrow of Richmond County. For £45 current money. 300 acres on a branch of Mountain Run called the Beaverdam ,.. corner to John Rennolds, Messrs. George and Thomas Fairfax land ... near a branch ... near a small branch ... as by Pendleton's deed 11 June 1749 ...
                          James Pendleton
                          Elizabeth Pendleton
   16 May 1751. Acknowledged by James Pendleton and Elizabeth his wife.

Pages 284-86. 18 Oct. 1750. Thomas Sparks and Mary his wife of Culpeper County to Ambrose Powell of same. For £25 current money. 200 acres in the Parish of St. Mark ... being part of a pattent granted to Richard Mauldin for 1000 acres in the hollows of the Great Mountains 24 March 1734 ... on a point ... on the river ... Zachariah Martin's upper line ... corner to Richard Mauldin ...   Thos. Sparks
                          Mary (X) Sparks
   Wit: P. Clayton, Wm. Stanton, Thos: Brown, Richard Thomas.
   16 May 1751. Acknowledged by Thomas Sparks and Mary his wife.

Pages 286-88. 18 Oct. 1749. Thomas Sparks and Mary his wife of Culpeper County to Ambrose Powell Gent. of same. For £3.18.- lawful money. 39 acres in the Robinson Fork ... in John Wilson's line corner to Sparks and Powell ... on the Robinson River side ... at the mouth of a branch ... part of that tract whereon Thomas Sparks now lives.
                          Thos. Sparks
                          Mary (X) Sparks
   Wit: Robert Coleman, Philip Clayton, Richd. Thomas, H. Field
   16 May 1751. Acknowledged by Thomas Sparks and Mary his wife.

Pages 289-91. 16 May 1751. Robert Traweek and Margery his wife of Culpeper County to Hugh French of Richmond County. For £112 current money. 750 acres, 400acres thereof was granted to Robert Traweek by a deed from the Proprietor's Office 22 July 1748 ... south side of the Hazel River corner to the land formerly granted to John Latham ... corner to William Nicholson on the river ... over a mountain ... the other 350 acres purchased by Robert Traweek of Christopher Strother by deed 22 Nov. 1746 ... corner to John Hughs and Thomas Stonehouse ... on the Hazel River ... on a point of rocks ... Hughs' line ...

Robert Traweek
Margery (X) Traweek

[   ]. Acknowledged by Robert Traweek and Margery his wife.

Pages 292-96. 17-18 July 1751. Francis Kirtley with Margaret his wife of St. Mark's Parish, Culpeper County, planter, to Robert Taliaferro of St. Mary's Parish, Caroline County, Gent. Lease and release; for £160 current money. 1459 acres in the Great Fork of Rappahannock River in the Parish of St. Mark's, being part of a patent 10 Sept. 1735 for 700 acres and Kirtley having obtained a warrant from the Right Hobourable Thomas, Lord Fairfax, Proprietor of the same, whereby there was found to be 1057 acres of surplus land within the bounds of the patent and desiring an including deed for the same which was granted him 12 June 1749 ... on a hill side on the lower side of a branch ... on the north side of Mountain Run ... crossing Mountain Run ... fork of a branch of the Mountain Run ...

Francis (P) Kirtlet

Wit: G. Hume, Thos. Brown.
18 July 1751. Acknowledged by Francis Kirtlet. Commission awarded for taking the privy examination of Margaret the wife of Francis. [Page 297 blank]

Pages 298-300. 18 July 1751. John Lacy and Anne his wife of Culpeper County to Nicholas Battaile Gent. of Caroline County. For £25 current money. 200 acres in the Gourd Vine Fork ... line of said Battaile's corner to John Manyfield on the Rush River ... in the hollow of a mountain ... said Battaile's line (formerly Mr. Francis Thornton's) ... being part of a deed from the Proprietor's Office granted to John Lacy 14 Aug. 1748 for 400 acres.

John (J) Lacy
Anne (X) Lacy

Wit: P. Clayton, Roger Dixon, Richd. Thomas.
18 July 1751. Acknowledged by John Lacy and Anne his wife.

Pages 300-03. 20 June 1751. Michael Clore and John Clore of Culpeper County to Paul Leatherall of same. For £20 current money. 100 acres in the Robinson Fork, being part of a patent granted to Michael Clore and John Clore 28 Sept. 1728 ... on a ridge ... side of a mountain ... a spur of the said mountain ... on a branch side ...

Michael (H) Clore
John Clore

Wit: Roger Dixon, P. Clayton, Wm. [W]illiams.
18 July 1751. Acknowledged by Michael Clore. Proved as to

John Clore by Roger Dixon, Philip Clayton and William Williams.

Page 303. 25 Oct. 1739. Samuel Parks of Orange County unto
Thomas Dillard of same. All actions, suits, dues, dutys and
accompts, sums of money and tobacco and all claimes and
demands whatsoever which in law or equity I, Samuel Parks,
against Thomas Dillard had and which I might have claime for
by any reason or means of my wife Mary Parks her right and due
share of her father Anthony North's estate.
Samuel Parks
Mary (M) Parks
  Wit: George Dillard, Michael Lawless, Edw. (d) Dillard.
  18 July 1751. Proved by George Dillard and Edward Dillard.

Pages 304-07. 17-18 July 1751. George Long of Culpeper
County to Martin Shirsh of same. Lease and release; for 5
shillings and divers other good considerations. Martin
Shirsh shall keep, take care of and maintain George Long and
Rebeckah his wife in good and sufficient meat, drink, washing
lodging and apparell suitable to their former and general
usage and condition of life during their natural lives and
also at their decease to bury them in a Christian like manner;
he shall not convey the land to any person during the natural
lives of George Long and Rebecca his wife but the same shall
be always subject as a security for their maintenance. 300
acres being the contents of a patent granted to George Long
28 Sept. 1731 ... on the ridge corner to Andreas Kirker ...
corner to John Huffman... a large rock on the Robinson River
side on the southwest side thereof ... corner to Matthias
Castler ...
George Long
Martin Shirsh [signed release]
    18 July 1751. Acknowledged by George Long.

Pages 307-08. 22 April 1751. Robert Frogit of St. Mark's
Parish, Culpeper County, blacksmith, to James Turner of
Hamilton Parish, Prince William County, planter. Mortgage to
secure £24 current money, to be paid within six months after
the date hereof. One full set of blacksmith's tools, some
iron and steel, one bed and furniture, one chest and all my
crop of tobacco hanging and striped in my tobacco houses, and
five head of hoggs which are marked with a crop and three
slits in one ear and underkeel and overkeel in the other ear,
and one black horse branded on the near buttock WD, one
bridle and saddle.
Robert (R) Frogit
  Wit: James Smith, Sarah Smith, Mary Turner.
  19 July 1751. Acknowledged by Robert Froggitt.

Pages 308-11. 19-20 June 1751. David Jones of Orange County,
planter, to Thomas Buckner of Caroline County, Gent. Lease
and release; for £188.2.6 current money. 350 acres in St.
Mark's Parish which by letters patent 1 June 1741 was granted
unto David Jones father of the said David Jones, which came
to him as heir at law of David Jones the father, deceased ...
on the south side of Stanton's River being a branch of the

Rappadan River ... corner to Thomas Stanton ... up the river ...
David (X) Jones
Wit: Roger Dixon, Richd. Thomas, P. Clayton, Wm. [W]illiams.
18 July 1751. Proved by Roger Dixon, Richard Thomas and William Williams.

Page 312. 18 July 1751. Bond of Francis Slaughter as sheriff of Culpeper County to render to the Auditor and Receiver General of his Majesty's Revenues a perfect account of all his Majesty's dues arising within the County and of all publick dues and fees put into his hands to collect. For £1000 sterling. Securities, William Green and Roger Dixon.
Francis Slaughter
W. Green
Roger Dixon
18 July 1751. Acknowledged by Francis Slaughter, William Green and Roger Dixon.

Pages 313-15. 18 July 1751. David Herndon and Mary his wife of Caroline County to Robert Covington of Culpeper County. For £30.7.6 current money. Tract in the Little Fork of Rappahannock River ... corner to Francis Thornton ...
David Herndon
Mary Herndon
18 July 1751. Acknowledged by David Herndon.
23 July [1751]. Commission to John Taylor, John Baylor and Richard Buckner of Caroline County, Gent., to receive the acknowledgment of Mary, wife of David Herndon, to sale of tract in the little fork of Rappahannock River.
12 Sept. 1751. Mary, wife of David Herndon, declares she was willing the same should be recorded.
J. Baylor
Richd. Buckner

Pages 316-17. 15 Aug. 1751. Michael Cook of St. Mark's Parish, Culpeper County, to Philip Snyder and John Carpenter, Junr., sons-in-law of Michael Cook, of same. For natural love and affection. 200 acres to be equally divided in quantity, in the Little Fork between the Rappadan and Robinson Rivers in St. Mark's Parish ... Philip Sneider's hundred acres to be joyning on the Island line on lands belonging to Henry Ayler and Christopher Tanner, it being the plantation whereon Michael Cook formerly lived whereon Philip Snider now lives ... John Carpenter Junr's hundred acres to be that part of the tract that joyns on the line of land that Michael Cook acknowledged to Christopher Krugler, it being 200 acres, the plantation whereon Frederick Beyerbeck formerly lived to be a part of John Carpenter Junr's 100 acres ... which said 200 acres is part of a patent granted to Michael Cook and Jacob Krugler for 400 acres 24 June 1726.
Mical Kuch [in German]
Wit: William Henderson, Abraham (A) Eddings.
15 Aug. 1751. Acknowledged by Michael Cook.

Page 318-22. 12 Aug. 1751. Francis Strothers of Culpeper

County and Susanna his wife, John Strother and Mary his wife to John Minor of Spotsylvania County. For £209.15.- current money. 1688 acres, one part of said tract being granted to Francis Strothers by deed from the Right Honorable Thomas, Lord Fairfax, Baron of Cameron, 27 July 1748, and one other part being 159 acres by deed 24 April 1751 and one other part of it being granted to John Strother by deed from Thomas, Lord Fairfax, 22 July 1748 ... near Captain Compton's corner on the north side of the north branch of the Rush River ... crossing the river to the mouth of John Strother's spring branch ... on the Flat Run ... John Strother's line ... on a point of Kennerley's Mountain ... corner of Thomas Kennerley's ... to a bunch of willows in Kennerley's great branch ... on the river bank at the mouth of a branch on the lower side ...

                              Francis Strother
                              Susanna (X) Strother
                              John Strother
                              Mary Strother
    Wit: Wm. Covington, Robert Covington, Thos. Baker.
    15 Aug. 1751. Acknowledged by John Strother and proved as to Francis Strother by William Covington, Robert Covington and Thomas Baker.

Pages 322-23. 16 June 1751. John Powell of St. Thomas' Parish Culpeper County, to Giles Samuell of St. Mary's Parish, Caroline County. For £27 current money. 400 acres now in his occupation ... in Robert Key's line ... up a mountain ... crossing several spurs of the mountains to the top of a ridge
...   John Powell
                              Janny (X) Powell [*sic*]
    Wit: William Barksdell, John Barns, Francis Slaughter Junr., James Sullenger.
    15 Aug. 1751. Proved by William Barksdell, Francis Slaughter Junr., and James Sullenger.

Pages 324-25. 16 June 1751. John Powell of St. Thomas' Parish Culpeper County, to Peter Sulenger of same. For £20 current money. 360 acres ... corner to Capt. Thomas Buckner on a point ... on the N. side Conway River ... on the side of Bushes Bluff ...   John Powell
                              Mary (X) Powell [*sic*]
    Wit: William Barksdell, John Barns, Frans. Slaughter Junr., Jas. Sullenger.
    15 Aug. 1751. Proved by William Barksdell, Francis Slaughter Junr. and James Sullenger.

Page 326. 19 Sept. 1751. Bond of Francis Slaughter as Sheriff of Culpeper County to render to the Auditor and Receiver General of his Majesty's Revenues a perfect account of all his Majesty's dues arising within the County and of all publick dues and fees put into his hands to collect. For £1000 current money. Securities, William Green and Roger Dixon.
                              Fras. Slaughter
                                W. Green
                              Roger Dixon

30

19 Sept. 1751. Acknowledged by Francis Slaughter, William Green and Roger Dixon.

Pages 327-29. 19 Sept. 1751. Francis Brown and Anna his wife of Culpeper County to John Mulheir of same. For £40 current money. 400 acres being the contents of a deed granted to Francis Brown from the Proprietor of the Northern Neck 26 Nov. 1746 ... corner to Coleman Brown on the Hazel River ... below the mouth of Hole Run ... head of a valley near a rock of stone on the So. West side of the Red Oak Mountain alias Green's or Moore's Mountain ... near a rock of stone on the south side of a spur of the said mountain corner to Coleman Brown ...
        Francis Brown
        Anna (A) Brown
 Wit: J. Lewis, Wm. [W]illiams.
 19 Sept. 1751. Acknowledged by Francis Brown and Anna the wife of Francis.

Pages 329-33. 17-18 March 1750 [1751]. James Pollard of St. Mark's Parish, Culpeper County, to Matthew Garrett of same. Lease and release; for £5 current money. 200 acres in St. Mark's Parish in the Great Fork of Rappahannock River ... near the old German road runing along a line pattent granted to Alexander Howard ... along a line patent granted to Horsnell to the road, then along the road to Finlason line ... upon the head of Draggon Run ... being part of a patent granted to Charles Stuart 28 Jan. 1733 and by Start transferred to George Home by deeds of lease and release in Spotsylvania Court 4 June 1734 and Home acknowledged to James Pollard by lease and release in Orange Court 20 July 1736.
        James Pollard
 19 Sept. 1751. Acknowledged by James Pollard.

Pages 334-39. 18-9 [sic] Sept. 1751. Thomas Kennerly and Mary Margt. his wife of Culpeper County to James Gillison of Caroline County. Lease and release; for £130 current money. 499 acres on the branches of Deep Run and Dovel's Run joyning to Bludworth and Amburger, being the land whereon Thomas Kennerly and Mary Margt. his wife lately dwelt ... in Samuel Coleman's line and corner to the land of Conrad Amburger ... on a knowl corner to John Paul Vaught ... corner to Joseph Bludworth now Capt. Roan's land ...
        Thomas Kennerly
        Mary Margt. (X) Kennerly
 Wit: Joseph Wood, Jonathan Gibson, William Barksdell, James Kennerly, John Gillison.
 19 Sept. 1751. Acknowledged by Thomas Kennerly and Mary Margaret his wife.
 [ ] Sept. 1751. Bond of Thomas Kennerly of Culpeper County to James Gillison of Caroline County. For £260 current money. To keep all covenants in indentures.
        Thomas Kennerly
 Wit: Joseph Wood, Jonathan Gibson, John Gillison.
 19 Sept. 1751. Acknowledged by Thomas Kennerly.

Pages 339-41. 19 Sept. 1751. Henry Downs Junr. of Augusta
County to John Rodgers. For £27.10.- current money.   115
acres lying at the foot of Neals Mountain and on the Rapadan
River joining Charles Neal's land ...
                              Henry Downs Junr.
   Wit: Francis (P) Kertley, Coleman Brown, John Deleny S.
   19 Sept. 1751. Acknowledged by Henry Downs Junr.

Pages 341-43. 19 Sept. 1751. Joseph Norman and Sarah his wife
of Culpeper County to Francis Browning Jur. of same. For £20
current money.   80 acres in the Little Fork of Rappahannock
River on the head branches of Battle Run ... on the side of a
mountain corner of Ashley's and Francis Browning's made on
dividing their land taken up in partnership ... on the top of
a mountain ...   Joseph Norman
                        Sarah (S) Norman
   19 Sept. 1751. Acknowledged by Joseph Norman and Sarah
his wife.

Pages 344-46. 19 Sept. 1751. Calem Price of Culpeper [County]
and Mary Ann his wife to Robert Eastham of same. For £13.2.6
current money.   264 acres ... in or near a line of Eastham's
land on a ridge corner to Thomas Dillard ... near the head of
a pond ... in a valley in George Dillard's line ... line of
John Lathum, deceased, near a small valley ...
                              Calem (X) Price
                              Mary Ann (/) Price
   19 Sept. 1751. Acknowledged by Calem Price and Mary Ann
his wife.

Pages 346-49. 19 Sept. 1751. Charles Neal and Hesther his
wife, Martin Dewett and Mary his wife of St. Thomas's Parish,
Culpeper County, planters, to James Herndon of parish aforesaid in Orange County, planter. For £53.15.- current money.
100 acres in St. Thomas' Parish on boath sides Stanton's River
... on the west side of Stanton's River right against the
plantation whereon Martin Duett now lives ... near a great
stone on a branch side ... Kirkley's line ... to a small
branch ... up the river ... including the plantation whereon
Martin Duett now lives ...   Charles (X) Neal
                              Martin (X) Duett
                              Mary (X) Duett
   19 Sept. 1751. Acknowledged by Charles Neale, Martin Duett
and Mary Duett his wife.

Pages 350-53. 16 May 1751. Frederick Fishback and Anaeliza-
beth his wife of Culpeper County to Peter Kamper of Prince
William County. For £15 surrent money.   100 acres in St.
Mark's Parish ... near the plantation where Charles Duett
formerly lived ... near a small branch ... near a small branch
...   Fredrick (F) Fishback
                              Analizab^h (X) Fishback
   Wit: Henry (H) Autuback, John (I) Butten, John (J) Crimb.
   16 May 1751. Acknowledged by Frederick Fishback.

18 May [1751]. Commission to Robert Eastham, Philip Clayton and James Pendleton, Gent., to receive acknowledgment of Anaelizabeth, wife of Frederick Fishback, to indenture of 100 acres to Peter Kamper of Prince William County.

11 April 1752. Analizabeth wife of Frederick Fishback did acknowledge the same.   R. Eastham
                                            J. Pendleton

Pages 354-57. 20 June 1751. John Wynill Sanders and Frances his wife of Culpeper County to Evan Thomas of Richmond County. For £25 current money.   335 acres ... on a small ridge on the south side of Butler's Swamp corner to Joseph Thomas Gent. and Robert Coleman ... corner to William Cowne near a path ... corner to Cowne on a ridge ... to a line of William Tutt ... on a hill side near a road of Capt. Robt. Green deceased ... side of a small branch corner to Robert Coleman... as by deed from Proprietor's Office 11 Dec. 1749 granted to John Wynill Sanders ...   John Wynell Sanders
                                      Frances (V) Sanders
   Wit: P. Clayton, Robert Coleman, Richd. Thomas, Wm. [W]illiams.
   20 Sept. 1751. Acknowledged by John Sanders.
   16 April 1752. Acknowledged by Frances the wife of John Sanders.

Pages 357-61. 18-19 Nov. 1751. Andrew Rosse and Daniel Campbell of King George County to Thomas Fitzhugh of Stafford County, Gent. Lease and release; for £190 current money. 880 acres ... line of Colo. Carter's Barron low ground tract ... by a branch ... Chism's line ... corner to Crim and Detherage ... Fishback's line ... corner to Detherage and Utterback ... dividing line between Dewitt and Green ...
                                      Andr. Rosse
                                      Daniel Campbell
   Wit: John Fitzhugh, William Cuninghame, William Harris.
   21 Nov. 1751. Acknowledged by Andrew Rosse and Daniel Campbell.

Pages 362-65. 18-19 Nov. 1751. Andrew Rosse of King George County to Joseph Hinson of same. Lease and release; for £60 current money.   372 acres ... under the Ragged Mountain ... on the north fork of Beaverdam Run ... the Widow Jones's ... in Spignal hollow ... in John Simpson's line ... granted to Andrew Rosse by deed from the Proprietor's Office 29 Jan. 1749 ...

                                      Andr. Rosse
   Wit: Thos. Hord, Daniel Campbell, John Knox.
   21 Nov. 1751. Acknowledged by Andrew Rosse.

Pages 366-69. 18-19 Nov. 1751. William Harris of Culpeper County to Thomas Fitzhugh of Stafford County. Lease and re- lease; for £25 current money.   183 acres ... corner to Capt. Green on the banks of the North River ... corner to Green and Tilman Weaver ... line of Pickett ... corner to Joseph Williams ...

                                      William Harris

Wit: Daniel Campbell, John (X) Shoemate, James Hurt.
21 Nov. 1751. Acknowledged by William Harris.

Pages 370-75. 23 May 1744. Butler Spotswood, Elliott Benger and Robert Rose, Clerk, executors of the last will and testament of Alexander Spotswood, late of Orange County, Esqr., on behalf of John Spotswood now an infant under the age of twenty one years, to Thomas Chambers.

Alexander Spotswood by his last will and testament 19 April 1740 recorded in the Court of the County of Orange did give during the minority of either of his sons John Spotswood or Robert Spotswood full power unto Butler Spotswood, Elliott Benger and Robert Rose as executors to lease any of his lands (except as therein is excepted) for term of years or for life or lives as he himself leased any lands in the Spotsylvania Tract in Orange County.

Lease of 150 acres in St. Mark's Parish on the north side of the River Rapidanne being part of 40,000 acres granted to Alexander Spotswood and called the Spotsylvania Tract.

For lives of Thomas Chambers and Elizabeth his wife.

Annual rent, 800 pounds of tobacco to be delivered in one hogshead at some convenient landing on Rappahannock River within Spotsylvania County, the first paiments to commence 25 Dec. 1747.

Thomas Chambers shall within four years plant 300 good fruit trees whereof one third at least to be good apple trees and the same well inclose with a good fence. Thomas Chambers shall not work the premises with more than six labouringhands.
                        Butler Thompson
                        Elliott Benger
                        Robt. Rose
    Wit: Henry Field, Alexr. McQueen.
    Survey of 150 acres ... on a stony point by Buck run ...
    25 Dec. 1744. Acknowledged by Elliott Benger and Robert Rose.
    22 Oct. 1747. Thomas Chambers of St. Mark's Parish, Orange County, to Richard Nalle. For 10 shillings current money. Assignment of 150 acres.
                        Thomas Chambers
    22 Oct. 1747. Acknowledged by Thomas Chambers.
    22 Nov. 1751. Richard Nalle of Culpeper County to Robert Taliaferro. For £17.10.- current money. Assignment of the within lease.
                        Richard Nall
    22 Nov. 1751. Acknowledged by Richard Nalle.

Pages 375-77. 22 Nov. 1751. John Shakleford, planter, of Culpeper County, to John Read, planter, of same. Lease of 150 acres, part of a tract whereon Shackleford now lives ... north side of south Branch of the Little Fork ... on a path side ... on Indian Run ... up the river ...

For lives of John Read, John Read junr. and Theophilus Read. If either of the lives should cease before 1820 the survivors shall have power to enter another life during the term.

Annual rent, 530 pounds of tobacco on 15 December.

If John Read or tenant work thereon more than four tithables besides himself, to pay for every tithable beside the four and himself 100 pounds of tobacco additional rent.

John Shackleford

John Read

Wit: John Wetherall, Harbin Moore, Tho: Houison.

22 Nov. 1751. Acknowledged by John Shackleford and John Read.

Pages 377-79. 17 Oct. 1751. Moses Botts of Fairfax County to John Gayle of Spotsylvania County. For £30 current money. 127 acres in the Gourd Vine Fork ... corner to Col. Francis Thronton, deceased ... the Revd. Mr. John Thompson's line ... on a hill ... by deed from the Proprietor's Office 1 July 1749 granted to Joseph Campbell and by Campbell conveyed to Moses Botts.

Moses (O) Botts

Wit: P. Clayton, Robert Coleman, Wm. Williams.

Pages 380-83. 18 Dec. 1751. John Spotswood of Spotsylvania County, Esqr., son, heir and devisee of Alexander Spotswood late of Orange County, Esqr., deceased, and Mary his wife, with consent of Butler Thompson, executrix, to Taliaferro Cragg of Spotsylvania County. For £60 current money.

[Provisions of will of Alexander Spotswood as in deed, pp. 243-47]

200 acres in St. Mark's Parish ... on Cedar Run corner to Alexander Mayfield ... line of Cragg's addition of his lott ...

John Spotswood

Mary Spotswood

Wit: Robt. Slaughter, W. Russell.

19 Dec. 1751. Acknowledged by John Spotswood Esqr.

19 Dec. [1751]. Commission to Robert Slaughter, William Russell and William Green of Culpeper County, Gent., to receive acknowledgment of Mary, wife of John Spotswood, to indenture to Taliaferro Cragg.

19 Dec. 1751. Mary, wife of John Spotswood, Esrq., did acknowledge the same.

Robt. Slaughter

W. Russell

Pages 383-86. 24 Sept. 1751. John Spotswood of Spotsylvania County, Esqr., son, heir and devisee of Alexander Spotswood late of Orange County, Esqr., deceased, and Mary his wife to Samuel Clayton of King and Queen County. For £60 current money.

[Provisions of will of Alexander Spotswood as in deed, pp. 243-47]

200 acres in St. Mark's Parish ... corner to Francis Gaines' lott ... in the low grounds of Cedar Run ...

John Spotswood

Mary Spotswood

Wit: Ben Pendleton, Ambrose Bullard.

19 Sept. 1751. Acknowledged by John Spotswood, Esqr.

2)ct. [1751]. Commission to Richard Tutt, William Hunter Anthony Strother and Charles Dick of Spotsylvania County, Gent., to receive acknowledgment of Mary, wife of John Spotswood, to

indenture to Samuel Clayton.
    12 Oct. 1751. Mary Spotswood acknowledged the deed.
                              Anthony Strother
                              Chas. Dick

Pages 386-89. 2 Oct. 1751. John Spotswood of Spotsylvania
County, Esqr., son, heir and devisee of Alexander Spotswood,
late of Orange County, Esqr., deceased, and Mary his wife and
Butler Thompson, executris of the last will and testament of
Alexander Spotswood, to William Williams of Culpeper County.
For £152 current money.
    [Provisions of will of Alexander Spotswood, as in deed,
pp. 243-47]
    510 acres in St. Mark's Parish ... at the mouth of Parks's
Branch on the north side of Mountain Run corner to Robert
Coleman ... south side of a branch ... Spotswood's line at
Parks' and Faver's corner ...
                              John Spotswood
                              Mary Spotswood
    Wit: John Weatherall, Edward Spencer.
    19 Dec. 1751. Acknowledged by John Spotswood, Esqr.
    20 Dec. [1751]. Commission to Robert Slaughter, Henry
Field, William Russell and Philip Clayton, Gent., to receive
acknowledgement of Mary Spotswood, wife of John Spotswood, to
indenture to William Williams.
    26 Dec. 1751. Mary, wife of John Spotswood, Esqr., did
acknowledge the same.   Robert Slaughter
                              W. Green

Pages 389-93. 18 Dec. 1751. John Spotswood of Spotsylvania
County, Esqr., son, heir and devisee of Alexander Spotswood
late of Orange County, Esqr., deceased, and Mary his wife,
with the consent of Butler Thompson, executrix of the said
last will and testament, to Alexander Waugh of Orange County,
Gent. For £81.12.- current money.
    [Provisions of will of Alexander Spotswood as in deed,
pp. 243-47]
    272 acres in St. Mark's Parish ... in the low grounds of
Cedar Run corner to Nathan Turner ... line of Daniel White's
lott ... in a glade of the Hay Stack Branch ... on the north
side of Cedar Run ...   John Spotswood
                              Mary Spotswood
    19 Dec. 1751. Acknowledged by John Spotswood, Esqr.
    19 Dec. [1751]. Commission to Rober Slaughter, William
Russell, Philip Clayton, William Green and Thomas Slaughter
of Culpeper County, Gent., to receive acknowledgment of Mary
Spotswood, wife of John Spotswood, to indenture to Alexander
Waugh.
    26 Dec. 1751. Mary, wife of John Spotswood, Esqr., did
acknowledge the same.   Robert Slaughter
                              Wm. Green

Pages 393-95. 3 June 1751. Henry Downes of Orange County to
Thomas Chew, Gent., and Timothy Croswait of same. For £60
current money.   300 acres being the reversion of 600 acres

granted to me by pattent 10 Sept. 1735 and also 150 acres which
I purchased of Anthony Head joining the same, the deed bearing
date 21 Feb. 1742 [1743] ... containing 450 acres, it being
the land where my plantation is on in Culpeper County.

Hen: Downs

Wit: Thos. Rucker, Edward (B) Brown, Cornelius Rucker.

18 July 1751. Proved by Thomas Rucker and Cornelius Rucker.

20 Feb. 1752. Proved by Edward Brown.

Pages 395-97. 20 Feb. 1752. Matthew Toole of Culpeper County,
planter, and Eliza: his wife to Joseph James of same, merchant.
For £100 current money. 100 acres in St. Mark's Parish in
the fork of Rappahannock River which was conveyed to Matthew
Toole and Elizabeth his wife by William Duff 10 April 1740 to
them and the heirs of her body begotten in lawfull wedlock and
by Matthew Toole and Elizabeth his wife was conveyed to Tully
Choice late of Orange County by a deed 27 Aug. 1746, and re-
conveyed by Tully Choice and Ann his wife to Matthew Toole 17
May 1750 by deeds recorded in the County Court of Orange,
the General Court of this Colony and the County Court of
Culpeper.

And 100 acres in St. Mark's Parish adjoining the above mentioned tract which was conveyed by William Duff by deed 24
March 1742 to John Brown and Jane his wife and the heirs of
her body begotten in lawful wedlock and by John Brown and
Jane his wife was conveyed to Matthew Toole by deed 26 March
1747 the entail being first lawfully defeated and cut off as
by deeds recorded in the County Court of Orange and in the
General Court of this Colony.

Matthew (T) Toole

20 Feb. 1752. Acknowledged by Matthew Toole.

Pages 398-400. 9 April 1752. William McDonaugh of St. Thomas
Parish, Orange County, hatter, to David Griffin of same,
planter. For £21.10.- current money. 150 acres, the remainder
of a deed granted to William McDonaugh for 400 acres 12 Dec.
1751 (the other part of the deed was sold to James Anderson),
near the Great Mountains on the branches of the Rappadan
and Robison Rivers and on the ridge between the rivers ...

Wm. McDonaugh

Wit: James (JA) Anderson, Thomas Smith, Zach Taylor.

16 April 1752. Proved by James Anderson, Thomas Smith and
Zachary Taylor.

Pages 400-03. 27 Dec. 1751. John Spotswood of Spotsylvania
County, Esqr., to John Thompson of St. Mark's Parish, Culpeper
County, Clerk.

By indenture 25 Aug. 1743 Butler Spotswood, Elliott Benger
and Robert Rose, Clerk, executors of Alexander Spotswood, Esqr.,
in behalf of John Spotswood, then an infant under the age of
twenty one years, did grant unto John Thompson 200 acres on
the north side of the River Rappadane, being part of 40,000
acres granted by pattent to Alexander Spotswood and called
the Spotsylvania Tract and by indenture 22 May 1745 the
executors did grant one other tract of 200 acres being part of

the tract of 40,000 acres to John Thompson, to hold the two
tracts for the lives of John Spotswood and Robert Spotswood,
yielding the yearly rent of 1000 pounds of tobacco, and John
Thompson having intermarried with Butler, the widow and relict
of Alexander Spotswood, who was entitled to a jointure of £500
sterling per annum as upon a deed of settlement upon the
marriage of Alexander Spotswood with Butler may appear, and
by an indenture quinque partite 23 Feb. 1746 between the
Reverend John Thompson of Orange County and Butler his wife,
late widow and relict of the Honourable Alexander Spotswood,
the Reverend Robert Rose of Essex County [and] Elliott Benger
of Spotsylvania County, Esqr., John Spotswood of Orange County,
eldest son and heir and devisee of Alexander Spotswood, Robert
Spotswood of Orange County, second son of Alexander, and
Anna Catharina Spotswood and Dorothea Spotswood, daughters of
Alexander, John Thompson and Butler his wife did make over
to Robert Rose and Elliott Benger a half of the annuity of
£500 sterling upon the trusts and confidence and purposes
therein mentioned much to the benefitt and advantage of John
Spotswood, and by a bond from John Spotswood and John Thompson
in the penalty of £2000 John Spotswood in consideration of
a deed of gift of half his mother's jointure made to Robert
Rose and Elliott Benger, did oblige himself to lease 400 acres
to John Thompson for lives for the yearly rent of an ear of
Indian corn, which land is since surveyed and laif off by
agreement in two tracts in some measure differing from the
limits and bounds of the first recited two tracts, and it
being the intent of the parties that the indentures of lease
dated 25 Aug. 1743 and 22 May 1745 shall be null and void, John
Spotswood for John Thompson's surrendering up and vacating the
two leases and giving up all his title to one moiety of the
annuity of £500, grants:
 230 acres ... on the Schoolhouse path near Robert Johnstones
fence ... on the south side of Mr. Lightfoot's road ... on a
branch side near John Thompson's fence ... east side of the
Courthouse Road and on the south side of a branch ...
 Also 163 acres ... on a point near a branch, corner to
William Nash's lott ... to the main road known by the name of
Bloodworth's ... corner to Thomas Watts Junr. now Robert
Spotswood ... corner to John Rawson ...
 For the lives of Butler Thompson his wife and William and
Anne Thompson his children.
                              John Spotswood
                              John Thompson
 Wit: W. Russell, Abraham Field, Wm. Eastham, Roger Dixon.
 16 April 1752. Proved by Abraham Field, William Russel,
and Roger Dixon.

Pages 404-05. 16 Jan. 1752. John Manspoil and Ann his wife
of St. Thomas' Parish, Orange County, planter, to John Day
of same, planter. For £30 current money. 100 acres of
woodland ground formerly purchased by John Manspoil of John
Sutton and by Manspoil sold to John Deer ... stake in a
branch ...   John (A) Molspy
                              Ann (X) Molspy

Wit: William Sawyer, Thomas (T) Burgis, David (D) Cave, John (J) Branham.
16 April 1752. Acknowledged by John Manspoil and Anne his wife.

Pages 406-09. 6-7 Sept. 1751. Samuel Parks and Mary his wife of Culpeper County to Humphrey Wallis of Spotsylvania County. Lease and release; for £100 current money. 388 acres in St. Mark's Parish on the upper side of Muddy Run ... upon Muddy Run at a corner of Kelly's land ... George Dillard's land ... Kavanaugh's line ...   Samuel Parkes
                                     Mary Parkes
   Wit: R. Eastham, Thomas (O) Howel, Thomas (X) Ridley.
   16 April 1752. Acknowledged by Samuel Parks.
   18 June 1752. Acknowledged by Mary the wife of Samuel Parks.

Pages 410-11. 16 April 1752. Daniel Brown of Culpeper County to John Wynell Sanders of same. Lease of 100 acres whereon Daniel Brown now lives, now in possession of Daniel Brown, by virtue of a lease granted by Elliott Benger Gent. and Robert Rose, Clerk, executors of Alexander Spotswood Esqr. unto Edward Teale for 200 acres ... to be laid off joining Mr. Robert Spotswood, Major Philip Rootes and Margaret Griffin's land including the plantation whereon John Sanders now lives.
   Yearly rent to Daniel Brown for lives of Edward and John Teale of 100 pounds of tobacco.
   John Wynal Sanders shall plant 150 good fruit trees whereof one third at least to be apple trees, have the same well fenced and trimed and maintain the buildings, orchards and fences in good repair and shall not work more than four labouring hands or so many weaker hands as is commonly allowed sharers in a crop.
                         Daniel Brown
   16 April 1752. Acknowledged by Daniel Brown.

Pages 411-12. 21 Feb. 1752. Bond of Thomas Rucker, William Rucker, William Offill and Shem Cook unto James Rucker and Ephraim Rucker, executors of Peter Rucker. For £1000 sterling. There have been several legacies delivered out of the estate to the several legatees: To Isaac Tindsley a Negroe boy named Yorkshire, to Shem Cook a Negro girl named Jenny, to Ephraim Rucker a Negroe girl named Phillis. If Thomas Rusker, William Rucker, William Offill and Shem Cook agree with the delivery of the legacies without taking any rents, interests, then this obligation to be void.   Thos. Rucker
                                     Wm. Rucker
                                     Shem Cook
                                     Wm. Offill
   Wit: Francis (X) Kirtley, Richard Vawter.
   21 May 1752. Proved by Francis Kirtley and Richard Vawter.

Page 412. 21 Feb. 1752. The subscribers hath received of James Rucker and Ephraim Rucker, executors of Peter Rucker, all of the estate bequeathed to me and my wife Margaret Tindsley by the said will, and discharge the executors of all

debts, dues and demands or any legacy to me or my wife
bequeathed by the will.　　　　Isaac (X) Tindsley
　　　　　　　　　　　　　　　Margaret (X) Tindsley
　　Wit: Richard Vawter, Wm. Offill.
　　21 May 1752.　Proved by Richard Vawter and William Offill.

Pages 413-15.　10 May 1752.　William Roberts of Culpeper County
Gent. to John Roberts, father of said William, of same, Gent.
For two young Negro men Charles and Tom and £10 current money.
400 acres being the uppermost part of a greater tract formerly
granted to Malcolm McKenzie by patent 20 May 1735 for 900
acres and a part of an including survey thereof made for 1500-
odd acres, all which lands was bequeathed by McKenzie in his
last will and testament to William and his brother John
Roberts Junr., lately deceased, which by John Roberts' death
descends to William Roberts ... in the little Fork of
Rappahannock River and on Battle Run and the branches thereof
... on the north side of little Battle Run, corner of land
Roberts formerly sold to Richard Young ... crossing great
Battle Run ... by a branch ... cross Great Battle Run again ...
Young's line amongst a heap of rocks and west side of Battle
Mountain ...
　　　　　　　　　　　　　William Roberts
　　Wit: H. Field, J. Pendleton, Benja. Roberts.
　　21 May 1752.　Acknowledged by William Roberts.

Pages 415-17.　5-6 Feb. 1752.　Jacob Kindrick of Culpeper
County to Joel Watts of same.　Lease and release; for £8
current money.　50 acres in St. Mark's Parish in the great
fork of Rappahannock River and bounded by a line that was
formerly Joseph Bloodworth's and by Frederick Cabler's line
and by the old Amelia Road that did formerly go from
Christopher Zimmerman's to Orange old Court house.
　　　　　　　　　　　　　Jacob Kindrick
　　Wit: Thomas Watts, John Hackley, Thomas Doggett.
　　21 May 1752.　Acknowledged by Jacob Kindrick.

Pages 418-21.　21-21 May 1752.　John Christopher of Orange
County, planter, and Anne his wife to Richard Bryan of King
George County, Gent.　Lease and release; for £120 current
money.　500 acres whereon Walter Fitzgerrald the Younger now
lives ... in the first fork of the Rappadan River bounding
according to patent granted to Elizabeth Battaley 28 March
1733 and bought by John Christopher of Moseley Battaley of
Spotsylvania, Gent., and the aforesaid Elizabeth his wife.
　　　　　　　　　　　　　John Christopher
　　　　　　　　　　　　　Anne Christopher
　　21 May 1752.　Acknowledged by John Christopher and Anne
his wife.

Pages 421-23.　18 June 1752.　Robert Stuart and Mary his wife
of Culpeper County to James Stevens of St. George's Parish,
Spotsylvania County.　For £40 current money.　200 acres of
woodland ground ... in the Reverend John Thompson's line ...
lines of Mr. Stuart's patent ...

Robt. Stuart
Mary (X) Stuart
    18 June 1752. Acknowledged by Robert Stuart and Mary his
wife.

Pages 423-25. 17 June 1752. John Quarles of Chesterfield County,
Gent., to the Reverend John Thompson of Culpeper County, Clerk.
For £200 current money.   300 acres in the Great Fork of
Rappahannock River being the equal half part of a tract granted
in partnership to John Quarles' father John Quarles and John
Ashley, both of St. George's Parish, Spotsylvania County, by
patent 6 June 1726 for 600 acres, the half whereof falling to
John Quarles as his father's nighest heir at law ... line of
a patent granted to the Honorable Robert Carter Esquire ...
which line divides this land from the glebe ... by a glade ...
                         John Quarles
    Wit: H. Field, Richard Young, Danl: Brown.
    18 June 1752. Acknowledged by John Quarles.

Pages 425-27. 20 June 1751. Thomas Jones and Catherine his
wife of Culpeper County to Robert Leavell of same. For £10
current money. 100 acres in the fork of the Robinson River at
the foot of the Lost Mountain ... being the contents of a deed
granted to Thomas Jones from the Proprietor's Office 3 Sept.
1750 ... hill side in Ambrose Powell's line ... crossing two
branches ... near a branch in William Croswait's line ...
crossing the mountain ... in a valley in or near Powell's
line ...   Thomas Jones
                         Catherine (X) Jones
    Wit: P. Clayton, Wm. [W]illiams, Beamont Sutton.
    18 June 1752. Acknowledged by Thomas Jones and Katherine
his wife.

Pages 427-29. 20 June 1750. Thomas Jones Junr. of Culpeper
County and Katherine his wife to William Griffin of same. For
£10 current money.   100 acres which Thomas Jones purchased of
Richard Mauldin on the branches of the Robinson River, part
of a greater tract granted to Mauldin by patent for 2500 acres
24 March 1734 ... by a branch side ... corner to Johnathan
Pratt ...   Thos. Jones
                         Catherine (X) Jones
    Wit: Richard Thomas, Beamont Sutton, Robt. Leavell.
    18 May [sic] 1752. Acknowledged by Thomas Jones and
Katherine his wife.

Pages 429-32. 8-9 March 1752. William McDonaugh of St. Thomas'
Parish, Orange County, hatter, to James Anderson of same,
mason. Lease and release, for £16.2.6 current money.   250
acres in St. Mark's Parish, part of a deed given to William
McDonaugh Dec. 1751 near the Great Mountains to be laid off
in square lines at which end of the land James Anderson shall
think fit to take it.
                         Wm. Donaugh
    Wit: Thos. Chew, Zach. Taylor, Thomas Smith.
    16 April 1752. Proved by Zachary Taylor and Thomas Smith.
    16 July 1752. Proved by Thomas Chew.

Pages 432-35. 6-7 July 1752. William Beverley of Essex County, Esquire, to William Russell of Culpeper County. Lease and release; for £10 current money. 200 acres in Brumfield Parish on the branches of Hedgman River ... on the south side of the North branch of Hedgman River ... Burgess' line ... on the road side by Stony Run ... on the side of a mountain ... up the courses of the river ...

W. Beverley

Wit: Tho: Harrison, John Field, Tho. Brown, Duff Green, Roger Dixon.

16 July 1752. Proved by Thomas Harrison, John Field and Thomas Brown.

Pages 435-37. 23 Sept. 1752. Anthony Scott of Culpeper County to his grandson Richard Burke of same. For love and affection. 80 acres in the North little fork of Rappahannock River ... in Anthony Scott's line on the south side of a Chestnut Branch ... corner to Thomas Corbin's ... up the south fork of the branch with Thomas Corbin's line (which is a water course) ...

Anthony Scott

Wit: Abraham Cooper, John George, William (W) Poe, James (IIIM) Wilson, Jas. Pendleton.

28 Sept. 1752. Proved by John George, William Poe and James Wilson.

Pages 437-39. 14 Nov. 1751. John Durrett of Spotsylvania County and Mary his wife to Philip Clayton of Culpeper County. For £40 current money. 390 acres in the Great fork of Rappahannock River being the contents of a patent granted to John Durrett 5 Aug. 1731 ... on a branch at the foot of Muddy Run Mountain ... up Muddy Run Mountain ... on the top of the mountain ... top of a ridge ... to John Asher Shaw's line ...

John Durrett
Mary Durrett

Wit: Moses (MD) Downer, Uriah Garton Junr., Richard Durrett.

22 Nov. 1751. Proved by Richard Durrett.

18 June 1752. Proved by Uriah Garton.

28 Sept. 1752. Proved by Moses Downer.

Pages 439-41. 20 Aug. 1752. John Frogg of Prince William County, Gent., to Michael Wallace of King George County, physician. Division of eight tracts to prevent survivorship:

The Right Honorable Thomas Lord Fairfax, Proprietor of the Northern Neck of Virginia, did grant unto John Frogg and Michael Wallace eight tracts in Culpeper County: 300 acres, 9 Sept. 1749; 1150 acres, 11 Sept. 1749; 1100 acres, 12 Sept. 1749; 416 acres and 143 acres, 24 May 1751; 315 acres and 103 acres, 25 May 1751; and 1931 acres, 27 June [1751], containing in all 5458 acres.

Michael Wallace shall enjoy five tracts: 300 acres by deed 9 Sept. 1749; 1150 acres, 11 Sept. 1749; 143 acres, 24 May 1751; 315, 103 acres, 20 May 1751, containing in all 2011 acres.

Michael Wallace doth agree John Frogg shall hold the other three tracts, 1100 acres by deed, 12 Sept. 1749; 416 acres,

24 May 1751, and 1931 acres, 27 June 1751, containing in all 3547 acres.

John Frogg

Wit: John Thompson, W. Green, Robt. Loury, Robert Coleman.
28 Sept. 1752. Proved by John Thompson, Clerk, William Green and Robert Coleman.

Pages 442-44. 20 Aug. 1752. Michael Wallace of King George County, phisician, to John Frogg of Prince William County, Gent. Division of eight tracts to prevent survivorship. [Terms as in the deed above]

Michl. Wallace

Wit: John Thompson, W. Green, Robt. Loury, Robert Coleman.
28 Sept. 1752. Proved by John Thompson, Clerk, William Green and Robert Coleman.

Pages 444-46. 20 Oct. 1750. Francis Browning Junr. and Frances his wife of Culpeper County to John Browning of same. For 10 shillings. 90 acres on the head branches of Battle run ... at the foot of a mountain ... according to Browning's and Ashley's patent to Hickman's line ... dividing line between Francis Browning and John Ashley ...

Francis (B) Browning
Frances (X) Browning

Wit: Samll. Scott, James Wade, John (J) Roberts, Philip Brashers, John (J) Smith. [Receipt and memorandum that possession was granted also witnessed by John (J) Coopper.]
15 Nov. 1750. Proved by John Cooper and John Smith.
19 Oct. 1752. Acknowledged by Francis Browning and Frances his wife.

Pages 446-48. 19 Oct. 1752. Courtney Norman of Culpeper County, planter, to William Strother of same, planter. For £10 current money [release; lease not recorded]. 100 acres, part of a tract patented by Isaac Norman and sold to Nathaniel Hillin ... line of the patent ...

Cortney Norman

Wit: William Brown, Nathan Nalle, Frans. Tyler.
19 Oct. 1752. Acknowledged by Courtney Norman. Mary the wife of Courtney relinquished her right of dower.

Pages 448-49. 19 Oct. 1752. John Powell of Brumfield Parish, Culpeper County, to James Rucker of same. For 5 shillings current money. 376 acres ... corner to Francis Conway ... over the mountain ... on the side of a steep mountain ... corner to Capt. John Frogg ... crossing the mountain again ...

John Powell

Wit: Thos. Rucker, Russil Hill, Bartholomew Vawter.
19 Oct. 1752. Acknowledged by John Powell.

Pages 450-54. 14-15 Oct. 1752. Adam Banks and Rosana his wife of King George County, planter, to Jeremiah Eirly of Culpeper County, planter. Lease and release; for £16.2.6 current money. 250 acres on the south side of Stanton's River joyning to the land of Leonard Stanton and Thomas Stanton,

Junr. and to the land of Thomas Stanton Senr. ... side of a
ridge ... corner to Leonard and Thomas Stanton Junior on the
river side ...   Adam Banks
                                          Rosana Banks
     Wit: Margaret Owens, Silent Simson, Ger^d: Banks.
     19 Oct. 1752. Acknowledged by Adam Banks and Rosana his
wife.

Pages 455-56. 19 Oct. 1752. John Wetherall of Culpeper County
to Richard Grymes of same, planter.   Lease of 100 acres
whereon Grymes now lives, part of a greater tract of
Wetherall's lying upon Huses River ... line formerly called
William Duff's old line ...
     For lives of Richard Grymes, Elizabeth Grymes, Thomas
Grymes.
     Annual rent 530 pounds of tobacco at the most convenient
landing on Rappahannock River. Richard Grymes will pay the
quit rents unto John Wetherall, build one dwelling house
sixteen foot square and one tobacco house 30 feet long and 20
feet wide, plant an orchard of 100 apple trees and the like
number of peach trees and leave the same well inclosed, nor
work above three tithes on the land.
                                  John Wetherall
     Wit: Wm. Williams, Richard Young, H. Field.
     19 Oct. 1752. Acknowledged by John Wetherall.

Pages 456-60. 19-20 Oct. 1752. Philip Clayton and Anne his
wife of Culpeper County to William Cowne, merchant, of King
William County. Lease and release; for £80 current money.
600 acres granted to Philip Clayton by the Right Honourable
Thomas Lord Fairfax by deed 25 June 1748 ... corner to John
Durrett ... on Muddy Run Mountain ... line of Messrs. Bryan
and William Henry Fairfax ... head of a branch in the line of
a patent granted to Colo. Henry Willis ... Walter Butler's
line ...   P. Clayton
                                  Ann Clayton
     20 Oct. 1752. Acknowledged by Philip Clayton, Gent., and
Ann his wife.

Pages 460-61. 15 Nov. 1752. Philip Clayton and Ann his wife
of Culpeper County to Thomas Graves of same. For £10 current
money.   90 acres being part of a patent granted to John
Durrett for 390 acres on the north end of Muddy Run Mountain
5 Aug. 1732 ... on a branch at the foot of Muddy Run Mountain
... on the top of the mountain ... in or near a line of a deed
granted to Philip Clayton from the Proprietor's Office for 600
acres, now William Cowne's line ... line of a patent granted
to John Durrett for 400 acres, part whereof is now held by
Walter Butler ...   P. Clayton
                                  Ann Clayton
     Wit: Roger Dixon, Danl. Brown, Richd. Thomas.
     16 Nov. 1752. Acknowledged by Philip Clayton, Gent.

Pages 462-68. 6-7 Nov. 1752. Mary Nicholson, widow and relict
of Thomas Nicholson late of Whitehaven in the County of

Cumberland and Kingdom of Great Britain, mariner, deceased, John Nicholson, eldest son and heir at law of Thomas Nicholson, and John Champe of King George County, Gent., to Samuel Donne of King George County. Lease and release, for £150 sterling. 1000 acres, part of 3000 acres granted to Henry Willis, Gent., by order of Council 20 Oct. 1730 and by Willis ordered to be patented in Thomas Nicholson's name.

Mary Nicholson and John Nicholson by letter of attorney 12 March 1750, recorded in the County Court of Essex, did appoint John Champe by the name of their friend Major John Champe in Rappahannock River in Virginia, merchant, their attorney to sell land in Spotsylvania County containing 1000 acres near the River Rappahannock as set forth in a patent to the late Thomas Nicholson 23 June 1732.

Mary Nicholson
John Nicholson
John Champe
Samuel Donne

Wit: Robert Jackson, Anthony Strother, Daniel Campbell, Willm. (W) Poe, Nathan Nalle, William McWilliams Jr., Roger Dixon.

16 Nov. 1752. Proved by William Poe, Nathan Nalle and Roger Dixon.

Pages 468-70. 7 Nov. 1752. John Spotswood of Spotsylvania County, Esquire, son and heir of Alexander Spotswood, Esquire, late of Orange County, and Mary his wife to Philip Clayton of Culpeper County. For £50 current money. 156 acres in St. Mark's Parish ... at the Mountain Run near Clayton's mill pond on the south side of the run corner to the lott of land laid of for Margaret Griffin ... near a meadow ... corner to Robert Coleman ... to Mountain Run ... which said land was laid off for William Gaines' lott.

Alexander Spotswood by his last will and testament 19 April 1740 did devise all his lands in Virginia to his eldest son John Spotswood and to the heirs male of his body and for default he gave the same to his son Robert and all his working slaves and their increase and gave his executors power to lease any of his lands (except his mine tract) and did also bequeath unto his son Robert £3000 sterling, to his daughter Anna Catherina £2000 sterling and to his daughter Dorothea £2000 sterling to be paid at their respective ages of twenty one years or day of marriage, to be raised by mortgage or sale of his lands, and appointed his wife Butler Spotswood (who is since intermarried with John Thompson, Clerk), Elliott Benger Esquire and Robert Rose, Clerk, executors, who are both since deceased and John Spotswood is now of full age. Since the death of Alexander Spotswood his daughter Anna Catherine hath intermarried with Bernard Moore of King William County, Gent., and his other daughter Dorothea hath intermarried with Nathaniel West Dandridge of King William County, Gent. The fortunes devised to Anna Catherina and Dorothea are due and it being found by experience that the growing rents and profits of the estate charged with the fortunes are not sufficient to raise the same, and it being thought more expedient to sell

part of the lands than to mortgage the same ...
                              John Spotswood
                              Mary Spotswood
     Wit: Roger Dixon, Nathan Nalle, William (W) Poe.
     16 Nov. 1752. Proved by Roger Dixon, William Poe and
Nathan Nalle.

Pages 470-71. 16 April 1752. Abraham Field, Gent., first
sitting Justice of the Peace for the County of Culpeper, to
John Lindsey, joyner, of Caroline County [Two indentures]
     Abraham Field doth bind out Samuel Pannil, orphan of
William Pannil of Culpeper County until Samuel shall attain
to the age of twenty one years, he being sixteen 8 August next.
     John Lindsey shall teach Samuel Pannil the art, mystery
and trade of a joyner, find him sufficient meat, washing and
lodging, and after the expiration of three years find him
sufficient apparel.   Abraham Field
                             John Lindsey
     16 April 1752. Acknowledged by Abraham Field, Gent., in
behalf of Samuel Pannil, orphan, and by John Lindsey and
approved by the Court.

Pages 472-74. 16 Nov. 1752. Francis Browning Junr. and
Frances his wife of Culpeper County to Courtney Norman of same.
For £75 current money.   180 acres upon the head branches of
Battle Run, being part of 400 acres granted to Francis
Browning and John Ashly by patent 19 June 1735 ... division
line between Francis Browning and John Ashley ... Hickman's
line ... top of a mountain ...
                              Francis (B) Browning junr.
                              Frances (/) Browning
     16 Nov. 1752. Acknowledged by Francis Browning and Frances
his wife.

Pages 474-76. 16 Nov. 1752. Francis Tyler and Anne his wife
of Culpeper County to Anthony Strother of same. For £40
current money.   400 acres granted to Francis Tyler by patent
20 Aug. 1748 ... line of Mr. Henry Tyler near the Rush River
and Peaked Mountain ... crossing the river ... high point of
Kennerley's Mountain ...   Francis Tyler
                            Anne Tyler
     Wit: James Kennerley, Francis (B) Browning, John George.
     16 Nov. 1752. Acknowledged by Francis Tyler and Anne his
wife.

Pages 477-78. 18 Jan. 1753. Jacob Barler of Brumfield Parish,
Culpeper County, and Mary his wife to Christopher Barler. For
£20 current money.   100 acres to be laid off out of a tract
containing 400 acres by patent granted to Matthias Smith 24
June 1726.   Jacob (J) Barler
                             Mary (X) Barler
     Wit: Roger Dixon, George Utz, Christopher Blankenbeker,
Matthias Wilhite.
     18 Jan. 1753. Acknowledged by Jacob Barler and Mary his
wife.

Pages 479-82. 21 Aug. 1752. John Spotswood of Spotsylvania
County, Esqr., son, heir and devisee of Alexander Spotswood,
late of Orange County, Esqr., and Mary his wife to William
Williams of Culpeper County.   For £282.10.- current money.
226 acres in St. Mark's Parish ... on the Rappadan River corner
to Capt. Anthony Garnett ... corner to Garnett and Christopher
Petty ... on the Robinson River ... to the forks of Rapadan
River ...
     [Provisions of the will of Alexander Spotswood as in deed,
pages 468-70]
                              John Spotswood
                              Mary Spotswood
     Wit: John Thompson, John Wetherall, Richard Young.
     18 Jan. 1753. Proved by John Thompson, Clerk, Richard
Young and John Wetherall.
     16 Sept. [1752]. Commission to Robert Jackson, Richard Tutt,
William Hunter and Charles Dick of Spotsylvania County, Gent.,
to take the acknowledgment of Mary wife of John Spotswood to
indenture 21 Aug. 1752 to William Williams.
     23 Oct. 1752. Mary, wife of John Spotswood, Esrq., did
acknowledge the same.   Richd. Tutt
                             Robt. Jackson

Pages 482-84. 15 March 1753. Robt. Trawick and Magery [Mar-
gery] his wife of Culpeper County to John McKenny of same.
For 1000 pounds of tobacco.   100 acres ... on the top of the
Red Oak Mountain corner to Mr. Francis Slaughter's land ...
line of a pattent granted to Daniel Brown ... south west end of
the mountain ... part of a pattent granted to Trawick for 400
acres 25 June 1751.
                              Robert Trawick
     15 March 1753. Acknowledged by Robert Trawick.

Pages 484-86. 27 Jan. 1753. John Farmer of Culpeper County
to Francis Browning of same. For £45 current money.   100
acres ... on William Duncan's line on the south side of Middle
Run ... on the river side ... to the mouth of Middle Run ...
                              John Farmer
                              William Duncan
     Wit: William Strother, John Duncan, Samuel Scott.
     15 March 1753. Acknowledged by John Farmer and William
Duncan.

Pages 486-87. 15 March 1753. George Moyer unto my loving son
Christopher Moyer. For paternal love, good will and affection.
100 acres ... corner to the said George Moyer ... George
Moyer's and Adam Broyl's line ...
                              George (X) Moyer
     15 March 1753. Acknowledged by George Moyer.

Pages 487-88. 15 March 1753. George Moyer unto my loving son
George Moyer Junr. For paternal love, good will and affection.
100 acres, part of a patent granted to George Moyer 24 June
1726 for 400 acres ... corner to said Moyer and Michael Kafer
on the north side of the Island Run alias the White oak Run ...

of Culpeper County, planter. For 100 pistoles. 200 acres
in St. Mark's Parish ... at the mouth of Rumsey's Branch on
the north side of the River Rappadann ... up the river ... on
the river bank at the Raccoon Ford ... by the road side ...
[Provisions of the will of Alexander Spotswood, as in deed
pages 468-70]
                          John Spotswood
                          Mary Spotswood
   Wit: John Field, Will Stanton, Moses Bledsoe.
   19 April 1753. Proved by John Field.
   17 May 1753. Proved by Moses Bledsoe and William Stanton.
   27 Aug. [1752]. Commission to Benjamin Grymes and John
Thornton of Spotsylvania County, Gent., to take the acknowledgment of Mary, wife of John Spotswood, to deed of 200 acres to
Peter Johnson 18 Sept. 1752.
   7 March 1753. Mary Spotswood acknowledged the deed.
                          Benja. Grymes
                          John Thornton

Pages 507-09. 21 June 1753. Matthias Smith of Culpeper
County to Matthias Smith Junior of same. For £20 current
money. 100 acres whereon Matthias Smith now lives in
Brumfield Parish, part of a patent granted to Matthias Smith
and Matthias Barler for 400 acres 24 June 1726 ...
                          Matthias (X) Smith
   21 June 1753. Acknowledged by Matthias Smith.

Page 509. 20 June 1753. Richard Breeding of Brumfield Parish,
Culpeper County, to his children Job, Ossamon, Ann, Abner,
Elijah, Druscilla and Richard Breeding. For natural love and
affection. Eight head of cattle, eight head of sheep, twenty
one head of hoggs, two beds and furniture, one horse and all
the rest of his movable estate, to be equally divided among
them when they arrive to lawfull age.
                          Richard (R) Breeding
   Wit: William Henderson, James Archer.
   21 June 1753. Proved by James Archer and William Henderson.

Pages 510-14. 14-15 June 1753. William Nash of St. Mark's
Parish, Culpeper County, to James Pollard of same. Lease and
release; for £20 current money. 200 acres in the Great Fork
of Rappahanock River in Saint Mark's Parish ... corner to
John Asher ... on the side of a hill ... line of Francis
Michals ... granted to James Horsnal by patent 27 Sept. 1729...
bequeathed to Francis Thornton Junior of Spotsylvania County
by the last will and testament of James Horsnal ... Francis
Thronton did sell the same to Thomas Pollard of Orange County
and Parish of St. Mark's by deed ... Thomas Pollard did sell
the tract to William Nash of Culpeper County.
                          W. Nash
   Wit: Danl. Brown, John Penn, William Pollard.
   21 June 1753. Acknowledged by William Nash.

Pages 514-17. 20-21 April 1753. Martin Nalle of Culpeper
County to John Gayle and Thomas Poole of same. Lease and

52

Wit: Elias Edmonds, William Jones, William Edmonds.
19 July 1753. Proved by Elias Edmonds, William Jones and William Edmonds.

Pages 534-36. 19 July 1753. Christopher Yowell of Culpeper County to Christopher Yowell Junr. of same. For £10 current money. 226 acres [sic] in Brumfield Parish, part of a patent granted to Christopher Yowell for 124 acres 12 Sept. 1733 as also of a deed granted to Christopher Yowell from the Proprietor of the Northern Neck for 80 acres 1752 ... on a mountain ... side of a mountain ... John Thomas's line ... side of Long Mountain ... in or near James Yowell's line ... James Yowell's plantation near his orchard ... on a ridge back of Christopher Yowell's plantation ...
                    Christopher (C) Yowell
19 July 1753. Acknowledged by Christopher Yowell the father.

Pages 536-37. 2 Feb. 1753. Gabriel Jones of Culpeper County to William Stringfellow and Henry Stringfellow of same. Lease of one water grist mill now on Indian Run, Gabriel Jones holds by virtue of a lease from William Beverley, Esqr.
    Yearly rent £6 current money on 6 June yearly, and to grind Gabriel Jones' corn toll free and hopper free.
                    Gabriel Jones
    Wit: Lucy Jones, John (X) Crawford, Thomas Wiatt.
    19 July 1753. Acknowledged by Gabriel Jones

Pages 537-38. 2 Feb. 1753. Gabriel Jones of Culpeper County to William Stringfellow and Henry Stringfellow of same. Lease of one water grist mill now on Indian Run, Gabriel Jones holds by virtue of a lease from William Beverley, Esqr.
    Yearly rent £6 current money on 6 June yearly, and to grind Gabriel Jones' corn toll free and hopper free.
                    Gabriel Jones
    Wit: Lucy Jones, John (X) Crawford, Thomas Wiatt.
    19 July 1753. Acknowledged by William Stringfellow.

Pages 538-39. 2 Feb. 1753. Bond of William Stringfellow and Henry Stringfellow of Culpeper County to Gabriel Jones, Gent., of same. For £500 sterling. Securities, John Jett, Christopher Hutchins and John Read of Culpeper County. To keep the mill in good repair.
                    William Stringfellow
                    John Jett
                    Christopher (C) Hutchins
                    John Read
    Wit: Lucy Jones, John (X) Crawford, Thomas Wiatt.
    19 July 1753. Acknowledged by William Stringfellow.

Pages 539-42. 19 July 1753. James Turner and Kerenhappuck his wife of Prince William County to Francis Browning junr. of Culpeper County. For £11.16.6 current money. 90 acres in the little Fork of Rappahanock River ... on the head branches of Battle Run in a line made between Francis Browning

and John Ashley dividing a tract of land by them taken up in partnership granted to them by patent 19 June 1735 ...
James Turner
Karenhappuck (X) Turner

Wit: Richard Young.
19 July 1753. Acknowledged by James Turner and Karenhappuck his wife.

Pages 542-43. 25 Nov. 1752. John Sampson, planter, of Culpeper County to William Robertson, planter, of same. Lease of 100 acres ... on the Run ... up a branch ... by the path ... Robertson's line ...
For lives of William Robertson and Mary his wife.
Yearly rent £10.3.- current money on 1 January, the first payment to be in 1754.
William Robertson shall work on the land only his own tithables.
John (J) Sampson
William (X) Robertson

Wit: David Davies, Richard (X) Mazey, Anthony (X) Head.
19 July 1753. Acknowledged by John Sampson.

Pages 543-44. 7 May 1753. Maximilian Berryman of Hamilton Parish, Prince William County, and Mary his wife to their two sons John Berryman and Benjamin Berryman. For natural love and affection. All interest they have in all the land lying in the first fork of the Rappadan River ...
Mexm. Berryman
Mary Berryman

Wit: Jno. Battaley, James (A) Archer, John Henderson Junr.
19 July 1753. Acknowledged by Maximilian Berryman and Mary his wife.

Pages 544-48. 15 Aug. 1753. John Triplet and Lucy his wife of St. Mark's Parish, Culpeper County, to William Green of same. For £44 current money. 44 acres, part of 515 acres bequeathed together with another tract containing 300 acres to John Triplet and his brothers Thomas and Nathaniel Triplet by their father William Triplet and Nathaniel having since his father's decease departed this life under age and without making any division, Nathaniel Triplet's part descended to John and Thomas Triplet who have since by their deed of partition July 1753 agreed that the 515 acres should be held by John Triplet and the 300 acres by Thomas, as by the will of William Triplet recorded in the County Court of Prince William and the deed of partition may more fully appear ... in a small branch ... on a bank of Mountain Run on the northeast side ... on the bank of the run opposite to the mouth of a branch which empties into the run at the upper end of John Field's land ... west side of the road ... along the road side ... crossing an old field ...
John Triplett
Lucy Triplett

Wit: Robt. Slaughter, Frans. Slaughter, James (X) Cummerford
16 Aug. 1753. Proved by Robert Slaughter, Francis Slaughter and James Cummerford.

Pages 1-7. 5-6 July 1753. John Frogg of Prince William County, Gent., and Elizabeth his wife to George Row of Culpeper County, planter. Lease and release; for £65 current money. 416 acres upon a branch of the Robinson River at the great mountains of Rappahannock River ... granted to John Frogg and Michael Wallace in joint tenancy by deed from the Proprietor of the Northern Neck's Office 24 May 1751 and by deed of partition from Michael Wallace to John Frogg 20 Aug. 1752 acknowledged in Culpeper Court 28 Sept. 1752 ... in a hollow on the north side of the Robinson River ... crossing the river ... near a steep bank ... line of a survey made by George Hume for Frogg ... south side of a mountain ...
John Frogg
Eliza. Frogg
Wit: Frans. (T) Tidwell, Findley (X) Machalaster, Joseph Morehead.
    16 Aug. 1753. Acknowledged by John Frogg.
    19 July [1753]. Commission to Thomas Harrison, John Crump, Anthony Seal and Henry Payton of Prince William County, Gent., to take acknowledgment of Elizabeth wife of John Frogg.
    14 Aug. 1753. Elizabeth Frogg acknowledged the deed.
Thos. Harrison
John Crump

Pages 8-10. 16 Aug. 1753. James Hume, orphan of William Hume, late of the Kingdom of Great Britain, deceased, to Roger Dixon, Gent., attorney at law and Clerk of the County Court of Culpeper.
    James Hume by the advice and consent of his mother Mrs. Sarah Hume doth bind himself an apprentice to learn the profession or calling of an attorney at law and scrivener or the trade and mistery of merchandize, to serve seven years. He shall do no damage to his master nor waste his goods nor lend them unlawfully, nor see damage done by others without giving notice thereof; he shall not contract matrimony during the term, play at any unlawfull games nor frequent bad company nor disorderly places.
    Roger Dixon shall use his endeavours to teach or cause to be taught the apprentice the profession or calling of attorney at law and scrivener or the trade and mistery of merchandize and shall provide sufficient meat, drink, apparel, lodging and washing suitable for an apprentice.
James Hume
Roger Dixon
    17 Aug. 1753. Acknowledged by James Hume and Roger Dixon. [Two indentures, one signed by each]

Pages 10-11. 20 Sept. 1753. Bond of Robert Slaughter as sheriff of Culpeper County. For £1000 sterling. Securities, William Green and Roger Dixon of Culpeper County.
Robt. Slaughter
W. Green

Roger Dixon
    20 Sept. 1753. Acknowledged by Robert Slaughter, William
Green and Roger Dixon.

Pages 11-13. 31 March 1753. Mosley Battaley to my son John
Battaley. For love, good will and natural affection.   500
acres in Brumfield Parish, all the remaining part of 1482 acres
granted unto me by patent 16 June 1738 ... bounded by a line
of John Rucker's land and lines of a patent for 500 acres
granted to my wife Elizabeth Battaley 28 March 1733 and a line
of 500 acres which I did give out of the tract of 1482 acres
unto my daughter-in-law Elizabeth Taliaferro and easterly to
the utmost extent of the courses of the patent of 1482 acres
into the main woods ...
                          M. Battaley
    Wit: Humphrey Wallis, Tho. Rogers, Roger Dixon.
    17 May 1753. Proved by Thomas Rogers and Roger Dixon.
    20 Sept. 1753. Proved by Humprey Wallis.

Pages 13-18. 10-11 July 1753. Alexander Campbell of King
George County to Thomas Fitzhugh of Stafford County, Gent.
Lease and release; for £190 current money.   880 acres ...
line of Colo. Carter's Barron low ground tract ... by a branch
... Carter's line where Chizems line intersects ... corner to
Crim and Deatherage ... in Fishback's line ... corner to
Detheridge and Utterback ... line between Dewitt and Green ...
                          Alex Campbell
    Wit: Roger Dixon, Mich. Wallace, William Cunninghame, R.
Bernard.
    19 July 1753. Proved by William Cunninghame.
    20 Sept. 1753. Proved by Michael Wallace and Roger Dixon.

Pages 19-21. 21 Sept. 1753. Bathsheba Bohannan, executrix of
Robert Bohannon late of King and Queen County, planter, to
Robert Tureman of Culpeper County, planter. For £20 current
money.
    Bathsheba Bohannon, by virtue of the last will and testa-
ment recorded in the County Court of King and Queen impowering
his wife Bathsheba (whom he made executrix to [sell] his lands
lying in Culpeper county ...
    200 acres in Brumfield Parish, part of a patent granted to
William Eddins and by Eddins transferred to Robert Bohannon
by deeds 25 May 1738 ... corner pine of John Eddins on the
top of a small mountain ... by a great stone on the side of
a mountain ...
                          Bathsheba (B) Bohannon
    21 Sept. 1753. Acknowledged by Bathsheba Bohannon.

Pages 22-24. 12 Nov. 1753. Jeremiah Early of Culpeper County
from Thomas Stanton and Lettice his wife of same. For
£98.5.- current money.   131 acres, part of a patent granted
to John Stanton and Thomas Stanton for 1000 acres 28 Sept.
1728 ... by a branch ... on the river ... bank of the river
against the Oatfield ... in the cornfield by a branch ...
Stanton's old line ...

Thos. Stanton
Lettice Stanton

Wit: Mary (X) Eddins, Josep (X) Eddings, Charles (X)
Peirson, John Early.

15 Nov. 1753. Acknowledged by Thomas Stanton and Lettice
his wife.

Pages 25-27. 14 Nov. 1753. Joseph Eddins and Mary his wife
of Culpeper County to Thomas Stanton of same. For £15 current
money. 200 acres, part of a pattent granted to Thomas Stanton
for 400 acres 10 June 1737 and left by will to Mary Stanton,
daughter of Thomas Stanton, it being that part of the tract
ajoining on William Kirtley and John Simpson ...

Joseph (T) Eddins
Mary (X) Eddins

Wit: Jeremiah Early, John Early, Charles (X) Peirson.

15 Nov. 1753. Acknowledged by Joseph Eddins and Mary his
wife.

Pages 27-30. 8 Aug. 1753. Thomas Stanton of Culpeper County
to Charles Peirson of same. Lease of land ... at the mouth
of the Wolfpen branch ... to the road ... on a ridge ... in a
little valley ... head of the lick branch ... on the river
side corner to William Peirson.

For fifteen years from 15 November next ensuing. Rent
yearly on the feast of St. Luke, 18 October, 450 pounds of
tobacco.

The tenant in possession shall not work above three
labouring tithables.   Thos. Stanton
Charles (X) Peirson

Wit: Spencer Haynie, Robert Turman, Francis (X) Harvie,
Nicholas (X) Holt.

15 Nov. 1753. Acknowledged by Thomas Stanton and Charles
Peirson.

Pages 30-32. 11 Jan. 1745. Thomas Stanton of Culpeper County
to Francis Harvey of same. Lease of land ... corner to
Jeremiah Early on the river ... to the Yellow Banks, a place
so called, to the patent line.

For twenty-one years from Micklemus next ensuing. Yearly
rent on the feast of St. Luke, 18 October, 450 pounds of
tobacco.

The tenant in possession shall not work above three
labouring tithables.   Thos. Stanton
Frances (X) Harvey

Wit: John Simpson, Joseph Ham, Spencer Haynie.

15 Nov. 1753. Acknowledged by Thomas Stanton and Francis
Harvey.

Pages 32-34. 16 Nov. 1753. Peter Fleshman of Culpeper County
unto my loving son John Fleshman. For paternal love, good
will and affection and 5 shillings. 200 acres in Brumfield
Parish being one moiety of 400 acres by a pattent granted to
Seraicas and Peter Fleshman on Burdyne's Run 28 Sept. 1728,
being the upper part thereof, whereon John Fleshman now lives,

also joining the land now held by John Thomas ...
Peter (F) Fleshman
Wit: James Graves, Alexr. McQueen, James Connor.
16 Nov. 1753. Acknowledged by Peter Fleshman.

Pages 34-39. 9 Jan. 1753. Francis Thornton of Caroline County, Gent., to Nicholas Battaile of same, Gent. For £66.13.4 current money. 1000 acres, part of 4452 acres granted to Francis Thornton by a deed from the Right honourable Thomas Lord Fairfax, Proprietor of the Northern Neck of Virginia, 1 Dec. 1751 ... at the foot of a mountain ... on the river ...
Frans. Thornton
Wit: Robt. Jackson, Jno. Thornton, Roger Dixon, John Dent, Humphrey Wallis.
20 Sept. 1753. Proved by Roger Dixon and Humphrey Wallis.
Whereas this deed being only proved by two evidences, have acknowledged it again before John Harrison.
Francis Thornton
Wit: John Harrison.
21 Feb. 1754. Proved by John Harrison.

Pages 39-43. 14-14 April 1753. Joseph Cotten of Culpeper County to John Barns of same. Lease and release; for £15 current money. 100 acres, part of a large tract granted by deed to Joseph Cotten on Thornton's River in Thornton's pass ... corner to Joseph Cotten's tract ... up the river ...
Joseph (J) Cotten
Wit: Robert Jones, Thos. Baker, Wm. White.
20 Sept. 1753. Proved by Robert Jones and Thomas Baker.
21 Feb. 1754. Proved by Wm. White.

Pages 43-47. 13-14 April 1753. Joseph Cotten of Culpeper County to Robert Jones of same. Lease and release; for £9 current money. 100 acres ... on the north side of Thornton's River and corner to James Cotten ... down the river ... corner to Francis Thornton ...
Joseph (J) Cotten
Wit: Thomas Baker, John Barns, William White.
20 Sept. 1753. Proved by Thomas Baker and John Barns.
21 Feb. 1754. Proved by William White.

Pages 47-51. 26 May 1749. Henry Sluchter [Slutchers in lease] to John Shafer. Lease and release; for £25.10.- current money. 200 acres, part of 400 acres granted to Ciriaces and Peter Fleshman by pattent 28 Sept. 1728 ... corner of the old pattent ... in Jacob Broil's line ...
Henrich Sluchter [in German]
Wit: Ludwig Fisher [in German], Henry Mickle (X) Moyer.
24 July 1750. Henry Sluder delivered this release unto John Shafer. Wit: Ludwig Fisher [in German], Henry Mickle (X) Moyer.
18 May 1752. Henry Sluder delivered this release unto John Shafer. Wit: George (GD) Mayer, Henry Sluder.
21 Feb. 1754. Proved by George Moyer, Lewis Fisher, Henry Slutcher.

Pages 51-53.   21 Feb. 1754.   John Parks of Culpeper County unto my loving son John Parks Junr. of same.   For 5 shillings and paternal love, good will and affection.   300 acres ... on Parks' branch ... mouth of a small branch ... corner to John Reynolds ... corner to Philip Clayton ... in John Spotswood's line ... to William Williams' corner ...
John Parks

   21 Feb. [1754].   Acknowledged by John Parks.

Pages 53-55.   21 Feb. 1754.   John Parks of Culpeper County unto my loving son Richard Parks of same.   For 5 shillings and paternal love, good will and affection.   100 acres ... at the mouth of a small creek corner to John Parks Junr ... corner to John Reynolds ... near the Court house road corner to John Favour and John Parks ... to Parks' branch ...
John Parks

   21 Feb. 1754.   Acknowledged by John Parks.

Pages 55-57.   12 Nov. 1753.   George Anderson of Culpeper County and Ann his wife to George Thompson of [   ].   For £14 current money.   100 acres, part of a pattent granted to George Anderson for 350 acres 10 Jan. 1735 in the Little Fork on the branches of the Rappadan River ... road above the plantation ... on a hill side ... road below the plantation ...
George (A) Anderson
Ann (A) Anderson

   Wit: George Eastham, Nathan Underwood, Thomas (T) Cofer.
   21 Feb. 1754.   Acknowledged by George Anderson and Ann his wife.

Pages 57-59.   15 Nov. 1753.   George Anderson of Orange County, planter, to Nathan Underwood of Culpeper County, planter. For £10 current money.   100 acres ... lower side of Elk Run corner to Thomas Coffer ... to a branch ...
George (A) Anderson

   Wit: George Eastham, George (X) Tomson, Thomas (T) Coffer.
   21 Feb. 1754.   Acknowledged by George Anderson.

Pages 60-61.   16 Jan. 1754.   Bond of Lewis Davis Yancey of Culpeper County unto James Pendleton of same.   For £50 current money.
   Yancey and Pendleton have taken up a tract of land in the Great fork of Rappahannock River adjoining the land of Robt. Coleman below Walter Butler's, and Yancey and Pendleton did agree that when a deed could be obtained from the Proprietor's Office that the land should be equally divided and the entry thereof to be made in Yancey name, which is done and a survey made by Mr. George Hume and found to contain 420 acres. Pendleton hath paid Yancey one moiety of the charges for warr[an]t, surveyor's fee, rights and pattent money.   If Lewis Davis Yancey shall convey to James Pendleton one equal moiety of the land or in case the same be sold to render to Pendleton one equal moiety of the money, the obligation to be void.
Lewis Davis Yancey

   Wit: William Roberts, Willm. Duncan.

21 Feb. 1754. Acknowledged by Lewis Davis Yancey.

Pages 61-63. 15 Nov. 1753. David Zachary of St. Thomas Parish, Orange County, planter, to James Zachary of Brumfield Parish, Culpeper County, planter. For £21 current money. 100 acres ... on the upper side of Elk Run on Thomas Jackson's line and adjoining to Thomas Jackson's line, William Crawford's line and Thomas Crawford's line ... David Zachary and Ann his wife hath hereunto set their hand ...
David Zachary
Ann (X) Zachary
Wit: Robt. Cave, William Bledsoe, John (X) Zachary.
21 Feb. 1754. Acknowledged by David Zachary.

Pages 63-65. 21 Feb. 1754. Thomas Watts of Culpeper County to Andrew Sheperd of Orange County. For £20 current money. 183 acres, part of a patent granted to Thomas Watts, deceased, and John Zacharie containing 333 acres, 17 July 1735 ... bounded on Bland Ballard's line, James Barber's and Dixon's lines ...
Thomas Watts
21 Feb. 1754. Acknowledged by Thomas Watts.

Pages 65-67. 18 Sept. 1753. Benja. Rush of Culpeper County to John Thomas of same. Lease of 100 acres, part of 400 acres granted to William Rush by pattent; William Rush dying without will and his son William dying without heirs of his body the land descended to Benjamin Rush as the next heir to William Rush the Elder ... bounded by the lines of Mr. Anthony Strother and Majr. Philip Rootes on one side ... down a branch ... on another branch at the ford ...
    For the lives of John Thomas and Betty his wife.
    Yearly rent on 1 January 475 pounds of tobacco.
    John Thomas shall not keep in constant working on the land any more than three tithables besides himself.
Benjamin Rush
John Thomas
Wit: [?; in German], Robert Mackie, George Row.
The rent to come due from 1755 and not before.
21 Feb. 1754. Acknowledged by Benjamin Rush and John Thomas.

Pages 67-70. 15 March 1754. Michael Holt of Brumfield Parish, Culpeper County, to Christopher Holt son of said Michael Holt of same. For natural love and affection. 122½ acres in the Little Fork between the Rappadan and the Robinson rivers in Parish of Brumfield ... corner to Michael Holt and John Broyl ... corner made by John Holt and Christopher Holt on the upper end of the dividing line between them ... Michael Holt's old pattent line ... part of a pattent granted to Michael Holt for 245 acres 28 Sept. 1728 ...
Mich. Holt [in German]
Wit: James Barbour, John (X) Holt, William Henderson.
21 March 1754. Acknowledged by Michael Holt.

Pages 70-76. 22 Oct. 1753. Thomas Kennerly of the Province of South Carolina and Mary his wife to Henry Gambill of Culpeper County. For £144 current money. 900 acres, part of which was granted to Thomas Kennerly by pattent 19 June 1735 and by a deed from the Right Honourable Thomas Lord Fairfax, Baron of Cameron, 8 Aug. 1749 ... in a large vale ... on a little hill ... top of a ridge corner to John Minor ... in Kennerly's Great Branch ... along Strother's line ... along the old patent line ... head of a little branch corner to James Kennerly ... south side of the Rush River ... head of a glade ...
                        Thomas Kennerly
                        Mary (X) Kennerly
    Wit: J. Pendleton, Jas. Kennerly, Danl. Brown, P. Clayton.
    21 March 1754. Proved by Philip Clayton and Daniel Brown.
    22 March 1754. Proved by James Pendleton Gent.
    22 Oct. [1753]. Commission to Robert Eastham, Philip Clayton and James Pendleton, Gent., to receive acknowledgment of Mary, wife of Thomas Kennerly.
    22 Oct. 1753. Mary Kennerly acknowledged the deed.
                        P. Clayton
                        J. Pendleton

Pages 76-80. 15-16 May 1754. John Shafer and Mary his wife of Culpeper County to Jacob Broyl of same. Lease and release; for £30 current money. 200 acres, part of 400 acres granted to Ciriacus and Peter Fleshman by pattent 28 Sept. 1728 ... corner of the old pattent ...
                        John Shafer
                        Mary (X) Shafer
    16 May 1754. Acknowledged by John Shafer and Mary his wife.

Pages 81-85. 1-2 March 1753. Isaac Smith, Mageret his wife of Culpeper County to Richard Vernon of Orange County. Lease and release; for £20 current money. 100 acres ... below the mouth of a branch ... to Beautifull Run ...
                        Isaac Smith
                        Magaret (X) Smith
    Wit: James Rucker, Ambrose Rucker, Richd. Thomas, David Harris.
    16 May 1754. Acknowledged by Isaac Smith and Magaret his wife.

Pages 85-86. 14 Feb. 1754. William Booton to Robert Cave of Culpeper County, planter.
    William Booton and Robert Cave having by pattent from the Proprietor's Office of the Northern Neck 15 Dec. 1749 obtained a grant for 204 acres in the first fork of the Rappadan River ... corner to tract granted by pattent to William Eddings ... Eddings and George Hume lines ... Robt. Cave's line ... corner to Thomas Duckworth ... lower side Smith's Run by the mouth of a small branch ... are willing to have a partition of the same:
    William Booton hold 114 acres ... on a branch side ... on Smith's Run ...
    Robert Cave hold the remaining part of the tract of land.

                         William Booton
                         Robt. Cave
     Wit: Elliot Bohannon, Jno. Battaley, Ambros Bohanon.
     22 March 1754. Acknowledged by William Booton and Robt.
Cave.

Pages 86-91. 1-2 March 1753. Isaac Smith and Margaret his
wife of Culpeper County to Richard Vernon of Orange County.
Lease and release; for £20 current money.   100 acres ... on
Robert Cave's road near the upper corner of Isaac Smith's
fence where Downer's path crosses the road ... mouth of William
Phillips' spring branch ... to Thomas Downer's line ... Robert
Cave's road ...   Isaac Smith
                         Margaret (X) Smith
     Wit: James Rucker, Ambrose Rucker, Richd. Thomas, David
Harris.
     16 May 1754. Acknowledged by Isaac Smith and Margt. his
wife.

Pages 91-96. 26 April 1754. Isaac Smith and Margaret his wife
of Brumfield Parish, Culpeper County, and Robert Harrison and
Frances his wife of Washington Parish, Westmoreland County, to
Richard Vernon of Brumfield Parish, Culpeper County. For
£105.10.7 farthing current money.   935 acres ... in Isaac
Smith's and Robert Harrison's line ... to Smith's Run ... corner
to Richard Vernon ... formerly a corner to Jonathan Finnell
now Richard Vernon ... on the south side of Cave's Road ... on
the north side of the main road corner to John Blewford ...
corner to Jacob Ward ... corner to Henry Downs ...
                         Isaac Smith
                         Margret (X) Smith
                         Robt. Harrison
     Wit: Jas. Walker, David Harris, Allin (X) Raines, Wm.
Pendleton, Edward Walker.
     16 May 1754. Acknowledged by Isaac Smith and Margaret his
wife.
     15 Aug. 1754. Proved by James Walker, David Harris and
Allen Raines.
     26 April 1754. Bond of Isaac Smith of Brumfield Parish,
Culpeper County, and Robert Harrison of Washington Parish,
Westmoreland County, to Richard Vernon of Culpeper County. For
£211.1.2½ current money. To perform the covenants in the
indenture.   Isaac Smith
                         Robert Harrison
     Wit: Jas. Walker, David Harris, Allen (X) Raines.
     16 May 1754. Acknowledged by Isaac Smith.
     15 Aug. 1754. Proved to be the act of Robt. Harrison.

Pages 96-99. 16 May 1754. William Roberts of Culpeper County,
Gent., and Jean his wife to Michael Lauter of same, yeoman.
For £15 current money.   100 acres in the little fork of
Rappahannock River and joining on the north side of Cannon's
River, part of a tract granted to Michael McKenzie, then of
the County of Orange, by patent 20 May 1735 for 900 acres,

which was bequeathed by McKenzie in his last will and testament to John and William Roberts ... bounded as by a survey made by Richard Young ... bottom of a deep valley on the north side of Cannon's River ... corner to said Roberts on the river ...

William Roberts
16 May 1754. Acknowledged by William Roberts.

Pages 99-102. 29 May 1753. William Beverley of Blanfield, Essex County, Esquire, to George Harding of Culpeper County, planter.   Lease of 100 acres where he now dwells, part of a tract called Ursulana, formerly surveyed by Robert Brooke, surveyor of Essex, ... corner to Jacob Waller's lott on Great Indian Run ... to James Spilman's tenement ... along Foxe's line ... leaving liberty of making a path or rolling road through the land where it shall be necessary for and desired by one or more tenants ...
For the lives of George and of his two sons Charles and George.
Yearly rent on 7 December, one Falmouth note for 530 pounds of top leaf tobacco, tied up with the same in small bundles.
If George shall work more than two tithables besides himself then to pay for each tithable over and above the two 105 pounds of tobacco additional rent.
George shall within two years plant an orchard of sixty four good apple trees thrity feet asunder from each other and keep the orchard well trimmed and cultivated within a good fence safe from cattle, horses, goats and sheep, and keep all houses in good repair.
W. Beverley
Wit: James Spilman, Thomas Hopper Junr., Richard Young, Sur.
20 March 1755. Proved by James Spilman, Thomas Hopper Junr. and Richard Young.

Pages 102-03. 12 June 1754. [George Moyer] unto my beloved son George Moyer Junr. For natural love and affection. All my stock of horses, cattle and hoggs with all my bedding, pewter, all my other household goods and all the working tools.
George (X) Moyer
Wit: Conrad (X) Delph, George (X) Slaughter.
20 June 1754. Proved by Conrad Delph and George Slaughter.

Pages 103-10. 25 Aug. 1741. Butler Spotswood, Elliot Benger and Robert Rose, Clerk, executors of the last will and testament of Alexander Spotswood, late of Orange County, Esquire, to William Christopher.
Alexander Spotswood by his last will and testament 19 April 1740 recorded in the Court of the County of Orange did give during the minority of either of his sons John Spotswood and Robert Spotswood full power unto Butler Spotswood, Elliott Benger and Robert Rose as executors to leave any of his lands (except as therein excepted) for term of years or for lives as he leased lands in the Spotsylvania Tract lying in Orange County.
Lease of 150 acres in St. Mark's Parish on the north side

of the River Rapadane, part of 40,000 acres granted by pattent
to Alexr. Spotswood and called the Spotsylvania Tract ...
     For lives of William Christopher and Moreton Christopher,
sons.
     Yearly rent 800 pounds of tobacco in one hogshead proper for
exportation at some convenient landing on Rappahannock River
due 5 Dec. 1744.
     William Christopher doth agree to plant 300 fruit trees,
whereof one third at least to be apple trees and the same
inclose with a good fence, and shall not work more than six
labouring hands to be full sharers in a crop.
                         Butler Spotswood
                         Elliott Benger
                         Robt. Rose
     Wit: Alexr. Waugh, Leonard Dozier.
     150 acres surveyed by George Hume: ... corner to Stephen
Wells ... to Cedar Run ...
     27 Aug. 1741. Acknowledged by Elliott Benger, Gent., and
Robert Rose, Clerk.

Pages 110-11. 15 Nov. 1749. I assign my right of the within
lease [that immediately above?] to Goodrich Lightfoot, Gent.
                         Thos. Jones
     Wit: John (J) Knight, Matthew (W) Knight, Jno. Bramham, Junr.
     8 April 1754. Goodrich Lightfoot of Culpeper County to
Mr. Humphry Wallis, merchant, of Spotsylvania County. For £60
current money.   The within mentioned lease.
                         Gr. Lightfoot
     Wit: P. Clayton, John Taylor, N. Pendleton, Wm. Gosney,
Robt. Coleman.
     17 May 1754. Proved by Philip Clayton, John Taylor and
Robert Coleman.

Pages 112-15. 20 June 1754. Christopher Yowell and Margaret
his wife of Brumfield Parish, Culpeper County, to Michael
Glore of same. For £80 current money.   400 acres in Brumfield
Parish ... in an old field corner to Jas. Yowell ... on
Coplands run ... corner to Michael Oneal ... corner to Peter
Glore ... corner to Michael Glore's ... corner to Nicholas
Crigler ...   Christopher (C) Yowell
                              Margeret (X) Yowell
     Wit: Richard Pollard, John Leavell.
     20 June 1754. Acknowledged by Christopher Yowell and
Margaret his wife.

Pages 115-18. 24 May 1754. Jacob Holtzclaw and Catherine his
wife of Prince William County to George Wayman of Culpeper
County. For £20 current money.   98 acres in the little fork
of Rappahannock River ... corner to Henry Huffman and John
Young's land ... by a spring a corner of Hamon Back's land ...
                         Jacob Holtzclaw
                         Catrine (X) Holtzclaw
     Wit: Jacob Spilman, Michael (X) Clar.
     20 May 1754. Acknowledged by Jacob Holtzclaw and Catherine
his wife.

Pages 119-24. 20-21 June 1754. Courtly Broil and Margaret his wife of Brumfield Parish, Culpeper County, to Michael Yager of same. Lease and release; for £50 current money. 100 acres in the parish aforesaid in the little fork ... south side the Robinson River in George Long's line ... in Matthias Casler's line ... in Laurence Crease's line ... up the river ...

Courtly (X) Broyl
Margret (X) Broyl

20 June 1754. Acknowledged by Courtly Broyl and Margaret his wife.

Pages 124-28. 20 Nov. 1753. Thomas Stanton of Culpeper County, eldest son and heir of Thomas Stanton, late of Orange County, and William Stanton of Culpeper County, second son of Thomas Stanton and brother of Thomas, to Zachary Lewis of Spotsylvania County. For £10 current money.

Thomas Stanton died seized of a tract on Stanton River and made his last will and testament 2 Oct. 1741 and did devise 200 acres on the south side of the river commonly known by the name of Guy Meely's to his daughter Elizabeth Stanton and did devise to his son William Stanton the remainder part of the land lying on the north side, being 200 acres. The will was proved in Orange County Court. By virtue of the devise William Stanton was seized of the land for term of his life, the reversion expectant in fee descending on and being vested in Thomas Stanton.

25 acres, part of the land devised to William Stanton ... on Stanton River corner to Stanton's land conveyed by Isaac Smith to Zachary Lewis ... at the mouth of Rockey Branch ... Stanton's line ...

Thos. Stanton
Willm. Stanton

Wit: Thos. Lendrum, J. Lewis, Z. Lewis Junr., William Chiles, John (X) Thurman, Nicholas (X) Holt.

22 March 1754. Proved by Thomas Lendrum and John Lewis.
20 June 1754. Proved by Zachary Lewis Junr.

Pages 128-30. 28 May 1753. William Beverly of Blanfield, Essex County, Esquire, to John Gouge of Culpeper County, planter. Lease of 100 acres where he now dwells, part of William Beverly's tract of land called Wakefield ... north side of the south river called Burgess River ... on the river bank near a clift of rocks ... by a rock stone ... surveyed by Richard Young, surveyor ... saving liberty of making a path or rolling road through the land where it shall be necessary for and desired by one or more tenants of William Beverly.

For lives of John Gouge, Mary his wife and Benjamin their son.

Yearly rent on 7 December at Falmouth or Fredericksburg, inspector's note for 530 pounds of tobacco tied up in small bundles ... If Gouge shall work more than two tithables besides himself, to pay for each over the two 105 pounds of tobacco additional, and shall not keep thereon any undertenant, shall plant an orchard of sixty four apple trees thirty five feet asunder from each other within a good fence.

W. Beverley

Wit: W. Russell, Robert Coleman, William (W) Poe.
21 June 1753. Proved by Robert Coleman and William Poe.
20 June 1754. Proved by William Russell, Gent.

Pages 130-32. 28 May 1753. William Beverly of Blanfield,
Essex County, Esqr., to William Poe of Culpeper County, planter.
Lease of 220 acres where he now dwells, part of William Beverly's
tract of land called Wakefield ... on the north side the south
river called Burgess River ... to the mouth of the river ...
up the Hedgeman River ... mouth of a branch ... surveyed by
Richard Young, surveyor ... saving liberty of making a path or
rolling road through the land where it shall ne necessary for
and desired by one or more tenants of William Beverly.
     For lives of William Poe, Lydia his wife and William their
son.
     Yearly rent on 7 December at Fredericksburg or Falmouth
Warehouse of 1000 pounds of tobacco. If Poe shall work more
than four tithables besides himself, for each to pay 200
pounds of tobacco additional, and shall not keep thereon any
undertenant, shall plant an orchard of one hundred apple trees
thirty five feet asunder and two hundred peach trees twenty
feet asunder, within a good fence.
                         W. Beverley
     Wit: W. Russell, Robert Coleman, John Gough.
     21 June 1753. Proved by Robert Coleman and John Gough.
     20 June 1754. Proved by William Russell, Gent.

Pages 132-35. 19 April 1754. Henry Gambill of Culpeper County
and Mary his wife to John Minor of Spotsylvania County. For
£91 current money.   571 acres conveyed to Henry Gambill by
deed from Thomas Kennerly 22 Oct. 1753 ... corner to Minor
and Henry Gambill ... James Kennerly's line near a branch ...
east side of Kennerley's mill road ... on a hill side ... line
of a tract formerly Francis Strother, deceased ...
                         Henry Gambill
                         Mary (X) Gambill
     Wit: P. Clayton, Thos. Baker, Wm. Williams.
     20 June 1754. Acknowledged by Henry Gambill and Mary his
wife.

Pages 135-36. 21 June 1754. James Strother and Martha his
wife in behalf of Daniel Flourey the said Strothers' son in
law, of Culpeper County, planter, to Jacob Spilman of Prince
William County, joyner.
     James Strother and Martha his wife do bind out Daniel
Flourey (of the age of sixteen years) unto Jacob Spilman as an
apprentice to serve his master untill he shall arive to the
age of twenty years.
     Jacob Spilman doth oblige himself to teach Daniel Flourey
in the art, trade and mistry of a house carpenter and joyner
and to provide Daniel with sufficient diet, washing, lodging
and cloathing during his apprenticeship and at the expiration
to give Daniel Flourey a sufficient set of carpenter's and
joyner's tools to carry on his business with and also give him
a suit of cloaths.

Jacob Spilman
James Strother
Martha (X) Strother
21 June 1754. Acknowledged by Jacob Spilman and by James Strother and Martha his wife.
[Two indentures, one signed by each party]

Pages 137-39. 12 Dec. 1753. John Wynall Sanders of Culpeper County to Robert Coleman of same.
.For £36.2.6 current money by indenture 3 Jan. 1749 Sanders sold Coleman two Negro slaves Mingo and Phillis and for 5 shillings did sell and mortgage a Negro boy Harry. John Wynall Sanders has since sold Harry unto Mr. Joseph James of said county. So much of the foregoing deed as relates to the mortgage is null and void.
In lieu of Harry, John Wynall Sanders for the better securing the title of Mingo and Phillis to Robert Coleman doth mortgage one Negro girl slave Luce.
John Wynall Sanders
Wit: P. Clayton, Danl. Brown.
21 June 1754. Proved by Philip Clayton and Daniel Brown.

Pages 139-44. 23-23 Oct. 1753. Michael Yager and Elizabeth his wife of Brumfield Parish, Culpeper County, to Thomas Poiner of same. Lease and release; for £40 current money. 200 acres in the parish aforesaid and in the Great fork of Rappahannock River, being part of a patent granted to Martin Walk and Tobias Wilhite for 400 acres 17 July 1736 ... on a hill side in a line of the patent near Teter Weaver's corner ... crossing some branches of Deep Run ... in Colo. William Beverly's line on the south side of the German Road ...
Michael Yager
Elizabeth (X) Yager
Wit: Ambrose Powell, Richard Vawter, Thos. Sparks, Russil [Russill in release] Hill.
21 Feb. 1754. Proved by the witnesses.

Pages 144-54. 25-26 June 1754. William Russell of Culpeper County, Gent., to James Hunter of Fredericksburg, merchant. Lease and release; for £44.18.1 current money. Mortgage of 388 acres in St. Mark's Parish in the Great Fork of Rappahannock River ... corner to Mutton Lewis ... Samuel Ball's line ... corner to John Hall ... Joseph Cooper's line ... granted to Peter Russell, late of Orange County, deceased, by pattent 23 Sept. 1728 and by Peter Russell sold to William Russell 21-22 July 1742 ... also one Negro slave Billy and seven feather beds and their furniture ...
W. Russell
Wit: William Taliaferro, Richard Waugh (Orange), Tho. Rogers (King George).
I agree the principal money of £44.18.1 shall not be called in or any suit brought against William Russell to foreclose the equity of redemption of the within mortgage premises untill 26 June 1756.

Pages 153-57. 13-14 Aug. 1753. Jonathan Finnal and Mary his
wife of Orange County to Richard Vernon of Culpeper County.
Lease and release; for £14 current money. 100 acres in
Brumfield Parish ... Thomas Downer's line ... at a road
called Robert Cave's Road ...

Jonathan (V) Finnell
Mary (J) Finnell

Wit: H. Field, James Isbell, Julious [Juliusin in release]
Christy.

15 Aug. 1754. Acknowledged by Jonathan Finnall and Mary
his wife.

Pages 157-62. 6 Aug. 1754. John Spotswood of Spotsylvania
County, Esqr., son, heir and devisee of Alexander Spotswood,
late of Orange County, Esqr., and Mary his wife to William
Armistead of Gloster County, Esq. For £950 sterling.

Alexander Spotswood by last will and testament 19 April
1740 did devise all his lands in Virginia to his eldest son
John Spotswood and for default gave the same to his son Robert
and annexed to the land all his working slaves, and did give
unto his son Robert £3000 sterling, to his daughter Anna
Catharina £2000 sterling and to his daughter Dorothea £2000
sterling, to be raised by mortgage or sale of any of his lands
(the mine tract excepted) and appointed his wife Butler
Spotswood (who is since intermarried with John Thompson, Clerk),
Elliott Benger Esqr., Robert Rose, Clerk, executors, who are
both since deceased, and John Spotswood is now of full age.
Since the death of Alexander his daughter Anna Catharine hath
intermarried with Bernard Moore of King William County, Gent.,
and his other daughter Dorothea hath intermarried with Nathaniel
West Dandridge of King William County, Gent., whereby the
fortunes devised to Anna Catharina and Dorothea are become
payable and it being found by experience that growing rents
and profits of the estate are not sufficient to raise the
same and answer the other purposes mentioned in the will ...

5389 acres in St. Mark's Parish ... on the west side of the
mouth of Thompson's Branch ... line of the patent ... crossing
the branch ... by a branch ... to the South Branch of
Rappahannock River ...

John Spotswood
Mary Spotswood

Wit: John Thompson, Mich. Wallace, Danl. Brown, H. Field,
Roger Dixon.

7 Aug. [1754]. Commission to Richard Tutt, John Thornton,
William Carr and Robert Jackson of Spotsylvania County, Gent.,
to take acknowledgment of Mary, wife of John Spotswood, to
indenture 6 Aug. 1754 for 5389 acres.

7 Aug. 1754. Mary Spotswood acknowledged the deed.

Wm. Carr
Rob: Jackson

15 Aug. 1754. Proved by John Thompson, Clerk, Daniel Brown
and Henry Field.

Pages 163-68. 7 Aug. 1754. John Spotswood of Spotsylvania
County, Esqr., son, heir and devisee of Alexander Spotswood,
late of Orange County, Esqr., and Mary his wife to Robert

Coleman of Culpeper County. For £235 current money.
   [Provisions of will of Alexander Spotswood, as in deed,
pages 157-62]
   270 acres on the south side of Mountain Run and 15 acres
lying opposite to it on the north side of the run, whereon
Robert Coleman now lives ... the 220 acres bounded as per plat
and the 15 acres bounded by the lands of Philip Clayton, John
Parks and William Williams.
                              John Spotswood
                              Mary Spotswood
   Wit: John Thompson, Michl. Wallace, Danl. Brown, H. Field,
Roger Dixon.
   15 Aug. 1754. Proved by John Thompson, Clerk, Daniel Brown
and Henry Field.
   7 Aug. 1754. Commission to Richard Tutt, John Thornton,
William Carr and Robert Jackson of Spotsylvania County, Gent.,
to take acknowledgment of Mary, wife of John Spotswood, to
indenture 7 Aug. 1754 for 220 acres in St. Mark's Parish.
   7 Aug. 1754. Mary Spotswood acknowledged the deed.
                              Wm. Carr
                              Robt. Jackson

Pages 169-71. 15 Aug. 1754. Charles Walker of Culpeper County
to Julius Christy of same. For £36.current money.   100 acres
part whereof is part of a tract which Charles Walker purchased
of Henry Downs by deed recorded in the County Court of
Culpeper and the other part Charles Walker purchased of Seth
Johnston in exchange for part of the aforesaid tract purchased of Henry Downs.
                              Charles Walker
   Wit: James Isbell, John Towles, Ephraim Rucker.
   15 Aug. 1754. Acknowledged by Charles Walker.

Pages 171-74. 6 Aug. 1754. George Moyer of Culpeper County
to Adam Broyl of same. For £60.18.- current money.   100 acres
adjacent to the land of Doctor William Lynn and Adam Yager at
the lower end of Moyer's tract on the White Oak Run on the
west side of the run and on the south side of the said Yager
Run, whereon he now lives, to be laid of[f] in an agreeable
manner as also all the surplus land in Moyer's patent adjacent
to the hundred acres as laid down in a plott returned to the
Proprietor's Office and surveyed by Philip Clayton. The
surplus with the 100 acres contains 375 acres.
                              George (G) Moyer
   Wit: P. Clayton, Robt. Coleman, Wm. Brown.
   15 Aug. 1754. Proved by Philip Clayton, William Brown and
Robt. Coleman.

Pages 175-78. 29 July 1754. Elias Powell of Culpeper County
to Zachary Lewis of Spotsylvania County. For £10 current
money.   224 acres on the head of the South Branch of Stanton
River ... on the side of a mountain nigh the head of the
branch ... side of a mountain ... granted to Elias Powell from
the Proprietor of the Northern Neck of Virginia 15 June 1749.
                              Elias Powell

Wit: John (M) McDaniel, John (X) Thurman, Henry Lewis, Junr., Mary Thurman.
15 Aug. 1754. Acknowledged by Elias Powell.

Pages 178-82. 15 Aug. 1754. Thomas Covington and Elizabeth his wife of Culpeper County to Samuel Henning of same. For £100 current money. 1165 acres which Thomas Covington purchased of Edward Teele for 950 acres as by Teele's deed in the County Court of Orange and is part of George Hume's Fox Mountain Tract and whereon Samuel Henning now lives ... Teele's line ... crossing the east side of Fox Mountain ... on a branch of Hungry Run ... by a small bridge on Bloodsworth's Road ... line of John Spotswood Esqr. ... corner to Thomas Wright Belfield, deceased ... on a ridge ...
                    Thos. Covington
                    Elizabeth (X) Covington
     15 Aug. 1754. Acknowledged by Thomas Covington and Elizabeth his wife.

Pages 183-90. 16-17 Sept. 1754. Alexr. and Daniel Campbells of King George County, merchants, to George Row of Culpeper County, planter. Lease and release; for £17.10.- current money. 150 acres on the Robinson River ... on the west side of the Pass Mountain ... side of a high mountain among some large rocks ... south side of the south branch of the Robinson River ... on the side of an almost unaccessible steep mountain and stony ... which was granted by patent to Alexr. and Daniel Campbells from the Proprietor of the Northern Neck 8 Aug. 1749.
                    Alex. Campbell
                    Daniel Campbell
     Wit: William Cunninghame, Humphry Wallis, John Mitchel, Danl. Fitzhugh, Thos. Lendrum.
     19 Sept. 1754. Proved by Humphry Wallis, Danl. Fitzhugh, John Mitchell.

Pages 190-94. 21 March 1754. Richard Downs of Culpeper County to William Stevens of Orange County. For £16 current money. 160 acres ... Samuel Taliaferro's line ... on the side of a mountain ... on an ivey point corner to David Jones and Richard Downs ... granted to Henry Downs and conveyed from him to Richard Downs and conveyed from Richard Downs to William Stevens 30 Aug. 1744.
                    Richard Downs
     Wit: Wm. Jackson, James Powell, Mark (M) Stowers, Isaac Smith, John Henderson, Michael Holt Junr.
     18 July 1754. Proved by Mark Stowers.
     15 Aug. 1754. Proved by Michael Holt Junr.
     19 Sept. 1754. Proved by Isaac Smith.

Pages 194-99. 19 Sept. 1754. Isaac Smith of Culpeper County and Margaret his wife to Zachary Lewis of Spotsylvania County. For £200 current money. Three tracts upon and near Stanton River, one of which containing 150 acres is part of a tract conveyed by Thomas Stanton Junr. to Isaac Smith 23-24 July 1740 ... corner to Jeremiah Early on the east side of a branch

of Stanton River ... corner to William Stanton ... Thomas
Stanton's line ... corner to Downs ...

126 acres adjoining to the 150 acres was granted by deed
from the Proprietors of the Northern Neck of Virginia to Isaac
Smith 1 Aug. 1752 ... Thomas Stanton's line now William
Stanton's ... on the top of a ridge ... on a mountain side ...
top of a mountain being the main ridge between the Robinson
and Stanton Rivers ... in a valley between the mountains ...

408 acres was by Proprietors by deed granted to Isaac Smith
... on a mountain ... on a ridge ... side of a hill at the head
of a valley ...   Isaac Smith
                                 Margaret (X) Smith
     Wit: J. Lewis, Humphry Wallis.
     19 Sept. 1754. Acknowledged by Isaac Smith and Margaret
his wife.

Pages 199-203. 19 Sept. 1754. Isaac Smith of Culpeper County
and Margaret his wife of Culpeper County to Zachary Lewis of
Spotsylvania County. For £110.12.5 current money. Two
tracts near the head of Stanton River commonly called Garth's
Springs, one 201 acres ... below Garth's Spring ... on the
side of a mountain on the side of Stony Mountain ...

306 acres ... line of Isaac Smith's ... side of a mountain
... in Mark Sower's line ... near Garth's Spring ...
     Which were granted to Isaac Smith by deed from the
Proprietor of the Northern Neck of Virginia.
                                 Isaac Smith
                                 Margaret (X) Smith
     Wit: J. Lewis, Humphry Wallis.
     19 Sept. 1754. Acknowledged by the parties.

Pages 203-07. 18-19 Sept. 1754. Isaac Smith of Brumfield
Parish, Culpeper County, to Benjamin Smith of same. Lease and
release; for 20 shillings sterling. 480 acres ... corner to
a tract of Benja. Smith's ... by a branch ... line of another
of Benjamin Smith's tract ... to a point of a mountain ... by
a branch ... on a ridge ...
                                 Isaac Smith
     Wit: J. Lewis, Humphry Wallis.
     19 Sept. 1754. Acknowledged by the party.

Pages 208-10. 16 Oct. 1755 [*sic*]. William Twyman and
Winnefred his wife of Culpeper County to Thomas Cofer of same.
For £9 current money. 10 acres joyning Thomas Cofer's
plantation ... on a run ... Cofer's former line up the run ...
bank of a run ...   Wm. Twyman
                                 Winnefred Twyman
     Wit: Nathan Underwood, Wm. (X) Bates, John (J) Pillow.
     17 Oct. 1754. Acknowledged by the parties.

Pages 210-13. 12 Dec. 1753. John Scott of St. Margaret's
Parish, Caroline County, Gent., to Joseph Wood and Elizabeth
his wife and John Scott Wood son of Joseph Wood and Elizabeth
his wife. For natural love and affection towards Joseph Wood

and Elizabeth his wife and towards John Scott Wood, son of
Joseph Wood and Elizabeth his wife and grandson of John Scott
and for their advancement.   400 acres granted to John
Terrall by patent 28 Sept. 1730 and by him conveyed to John
Scott on the records of Orange County ... on the north side of
the Rappadan River corner to Thomas Scott ... on a hill ...
line of Colo. John Grymes's ...

John Scott

  Wit: Johnny Scott, John Crittenden, Jas. (X) White, Mary
Scott, Thos. Scott, Thos. (T) Tadbock, Alexander (AH) Henderson,
Nathl. Gear, Edwd. (E) Hanm.
  16 Aug. 1754. Proved by Thomas Scott Gent. and Nathl. Gear.
  21 Nov. 1754. Proved by John Crittenden.

Pages 213-16. 21 Nov. 1754. William Green of Culpeper County
to Daniel Duvall of Caroline County.   Lease of 200 acres,
part of a larger tract near the Ragged Mountain ... on the
south side of Hughes's River being a corner between the land
of William Green and Robert Green ... on Landrum's Run ...
land of Nicholas Green ... to Robert Green's line ...
  Yearly rent on 1 January, 1060 pounds of tobacco to be
delivered at Falmouth, Fredericksburg or Royston's Warehouse.
  If Daniel shall work more than seven tithables on the land,
to pay for every tithable beside the seven 100 pounds of
tobacco additional rent.
  For seven years or during the life of any person whom
Daniel Duvall shall think fit.
  Daniel Duvall shall keep an orchard of apple trees with one
hundred and fifty trees free from cattle, horses, sheep and
goats.

W. Green

  21 Nov. 1754. Acknowledged by William Green, Gent.

Pages 216-19. 21 [   ] 1754. James Kennerly and Elizabeth
his wife of Brumfield Parish, Culpeper County, to Henry
Gambill of same. For £10 current money.   200 acres ... on a
point of Mount delamore [?] ... on a point of Kennerly's
Mountain ...

James Kennerly

  21 Nov. 1754. Acknowledged by the party.

Pages 219-23. 17 Jan. 1755. William Tapp of St. Mark's Parish,
Culpeper County, planter, to my three loving children, my son
William Tapp, my son Vincent Tapp and my daughter Sarah who
lately intermarried John Jett, all of same, planters. For
natural love, good will and affection.   Land in the Little
Fork of Rappahannock River on Deatherage's Run and the
branches thereof, bounded as by a survey made by Richard Young,
a surveyor ...
  For my son William Tapp ... on the north side of Deatherage's
Run ... up a small branch ... Colo. Willis's line ... by
Duett's Road ... in Frederick Fishback's line ... crossing
Deatherage's Run ... at the great fork of the run ... 143 acres.
  For my son Vincent Tapp ... north side the run corner to
his brother Wm. Tapp's land ... up the south branch ... up the

main north branch ... corner in Jacob Holtzclaw's line ... 204 acres.

For my well beloved daughter Sarah Jett and her husband John Jett ... corner to the land given to Vincent Tapp on the south side a branch of Deatherage's Run ... corner to Fishback ... line of the patent ... 148 acres.
                              William Tapp
    Wit: Wm. Eastham, John Eastham, Robert Eastham jr.
    20 March 1755. Acknowledged by the party.

Pages 223-29. 21-20 Dec. 1754. Benjamin Rush of Culpeper County and Rachel his wife to Philip Rootes of Stratton Major Parish, King and Queen County. Lease and release, for £150 current money. 300 acres being the plantation whereon Benja. Rush now liveth, adjoining to the land of Philip Rootes and is part of 400 acres granted to William Rush, father to Benjamin ... on a ivy point by the river side ... by a run side ...   Benjamin Rush
                              Rachel Rush
    Wit: John Scott, Thomas Griffin, John Kelly, James Rush.
    20 March 1755. Acknowledged by the parties. Rachel was first privily examined.

Pages 229-31. 24 Dec. 1754. John Thomas of Culpeper County to Philip Rootes of King and Queen County, Gent.

By lease 18 Sept. 1753 between Benja. Rush of Culpeper County and John Thomas of same, Benjamin granted to John Thomas 100 acres, part of 400 acres formerly granted to Wm. Rush by pattent ... bounded by the lines of Mr. Anthony Strother and Philip Rootes on one side the needorona Branch that heads up to a line of Philip Rootes ... another branch ... for the lives of John Thomas and Betty his wife at the yearly rent of 475 pounds of tobacco. Philip Rootes hath contracted for the assignment of the land for £20 current money.
                              John Thomas
    Wit: John Scott, John Clore, James Rush, John (X) Rush, Simon Haniker [Kanitzer?].
    20 March 1755. Proved by John Scott, Simon Haniker, and John Clore.

Pages 231-35. 20 March 1755. Peter Sullenger of Culpeper County and Elizabeth his wife to James Macginis of Orange County. For £36 current money. 360 acres upon Stanton and Conway Rivers granted by the Proprietor of the Northern Neck of Virginia by deed 14 June 1751 unto John Powell of Culpeper County and by John Powell sold 16 June 1751 to Peter Sullenger ... corner to Capt. Thomas Buckner's on a point ... on the north side Conway River ... on the side of Blushes Bluff ...   Peter Sullenger
                              Elizabeth (X) Sullenger
    20 March 1755. Acknowledged by the parties. Elizabeth was first privily examined.

Pages 235-41. 14-15 Feb. 1755. George Hume of Culpeper

County to Henry Elly of same. Lease and release; for £61.10.0 current money. 1749 acres in the Great Fork of Rappahannock River, 723 acres thereof being formerly acknowledged to Henry Elly in Orange Court by deeds of leave and release 24 Feb. 1728 [1748 in release] and the remainder, 1023 acres, joining to the same and being part of a greater tract belonging to George Hume ... on the Meander Run on the north side corner of a tract of land formerly granted by pattent to James Kirtly now in the possession of Richard Barnes of Richmond County ... in a valley corner to Samuel Henning ... where Bloodworth's Road crosses the run ... the road in Colo. John Spotswood's line ... Mr. Richard Barns' corner ...
G. Hume
    Wit: H. Field, Alexr. McQueen, Wm. Stanton, Joseph Rosson.
    15 Feb. 1755. Receipt witnessed by Robert Waeit, Sharshall Grasty.
    20 March 1755. Proved by Henry Field, Alexander McQueen and Joseph Rosson.

Pages 242-46. 24-25 Oct. 1753. George Hume of Culpeper County to Francis Hume of same. Lease and release; for £20 current money. 100 acres, part of a pattent granted to Goodrich Lightfoot for 446 acres 13 June 1726 in the Great Fork of Rappahannock River ... in Stanton's line ...
G. Hume
    Wit: H. Field, Joseph Rosson, Henry Field junr., William Stanton.
    20 March 1755. Proved by Henry Field, Joseph Rosson and Henry Field Junr.

Pages 246-53. 21-20 Feb. 1754. Humphry Wallis of Spotsylvania County, Gent., to Christopher Homes of Culpeper County, Gent. Lease and release; for 17,000 pounds of tobacco. 380 acres in St. Mark's Parish on the upper side of Muddy Run ... corner of Kelly's land ... George Dillard's land ... Kavanaugh's line ...
Humphry Wallis
    Wit: Robert Coleman, John Yancey, Richard Pollard, W. Robertson.
    20 March 1755. Proved by Robert Coleman, John Yancey and William Robertson.

Pages 253-55. 10 March 1755. John Powell of Brumfield Parish, Culpeper County, to Bartholomew Vawter of same. For £15 current money. 100 acres in Brumfield Parish ... line of a patent granted to John Rucker ... corner to William Eddings ... corner to George Eastham ... Thomas Rucker's lines ... his wife Mary Powell [will] relinquish her right of dower.
John Powell
    Wit: Jeremiah Pearce, John Offill, Thomas Freeman, David Vawter.
    20 March 1755. Acknowledged by the party.

Pages 256-60. 21-20 March 1755. John Powell and Mary his wife of Culpeper County to Francis Kirtley of same. Lease and release; for £100 current money.   1012 acres ... on the head of a branch of Garth's Run and corner to Capt. Thomas Buckner's ... on the ridge of a mountain ... on the side of Bushes Bluff ... line of another survey of Powell

and ... line of Isaac Smith ... corner to Smith, David Jones and Robert Key ... on Garth's run ... mouth of a branch ... Powell's line ...   John Powell
                                Mary (O) Powell
    Wit: Thos. Stanton, Micajah Pickett, Elias Powell, William Kirtley, Thomas Kirtley.
    20 March 1755.   Acknowledged by the parties.

Pages 260-61.   20 March 1755.   William Lobb of Louisa County and Catherine Lobb his wife to Vivion Daniel of Orange County. For £100 current money.   150 acres ... in the Gourd Vine Fork on the north side the south fork Gourd Vine called the Hazel River ... Martin Nalle's line ...
                                William Lobb
                                Catherine (X) Lobb
    Wit: John Towles, James Johnson, John Brown.
    20 March 1755.   Acknowledged by the parties.   Catherine was first privily examined.

Pages 264-69.   14-15 Aug. 1754.   John Frogg of Hamilton Parish, Prince William County, Gent., and Elizabeth his wife, to Christopher Owel of Brumfield Parish, Culpeper County.   Lease and release; for £60 current money.   511 acres in Brumfield Parish at the Great Mountains on the north side of the North Branch of the Robinson River ... part of 1100 acres taken up in joint tenantcy by John Frogg and Michael Wallace of King George County, physician, by deed from the Proprietor's Office 12 Sept. 1749 and by deeds of partition between Michael Wallace and John Frogg 20 Aug. 1752 admitted to record in Culpeper County Court 28 Sept. 1752, by virtue of which the tract of 1100 acres became the property of John Frogg ... on the east side of the North Branch of Robinson River under a steep cliff ... to Major Philip Rootes' line ... on a branch ...
                                John Frogg
                                Eliza. Frogg
    Wit: John Wright, John Crump, Joseph Morehead.
    20 March 1755.   Acknowledged by John.
    25 Jan. [1755].   Commission to John Wright, John Crump and Elias Edmonds of Prince William County, Gent., to take acknowledgment of Elizabeth wife of John Frogg.
    10 Feb. 1755.   Eliza, wife of John Frogg, relinquished her right of dower.   John Wright
                                John Crump

Pages 269-70.   28 Feb. 1755.   Alexander McQueen of Culpeper County to my son John McQueen.   For love, good will and natural affection.   200 acres in St. Mark's Parish ... on a stony point corner to Richard Tutt, Gent., in John Yancey's line ... Alexander McQueen's line ...
                                Alexr. McQueen
    20 March 1755.   Acknowledged by the party.

Pages 270-72. 16 Jan. 1755. Jacob Medley and Elizabeth his wife of Brumfield Parish, Culpeper County, to Charles Brooking of same. For £5 current money. 50 acres, the upper part of that tract of land whereon Jacob Medley and Elizabeth his wife now dwelleth ... line that divideth Jacob Medley's land from the land of May Burton's standing in Grymes' Run ... land formerly belonging to John Terrell at the foot of the Lost Mountain ... head of a branch near the foot of the Lost Mountain corner to Medley, Terrill and Barnett ...

Jacob Medley
Eliza. (X) Medley

Wit: Stockly Towles, John (X) Layton.
20 March 1755. Acknowledged by the parties. Elizabeth was first privily examined.

Pages 272-74. 16 Jan. 1755. May Burton and Hannah his wife of Brumfield Parish, Culpeper County, to Charles Brooking of same. For £25 current money. 100 acres, the upper part of the tract of land whereon I now live ... in Grymes' Run now corner to Jacob Medley ... John Medley's line on a hill ... on a branch side ...

May Burton
Hannah (X) Burton

Wit: Stokly Towles, John (X) Layton.
20 March 1753. Acknowledged by the parties. Hannah was first privily examined.

Pages 275-77. 16 Jan. 1755. May Burton and Hannah his wife of Brumfield Parish, Culpeper County, to Jacob Medley of same. For £15 current money. 200 acres, the lower part of that tract of land whereon May Burton and Hannah his wife now dwelleth in the parish aforesaid ... Medley's line standing in Grymes' Run ... Col. Grymes' line ... corner to Jacob Medley ...

May Burton
Hannah (X) Burton

Wit: Stokly Towles, John (X) Layton.
20 March 1755. Acknowledged by parties. Hannah was first privily examined.

Pages 277-82. 13 Feb. 1755. Robert Covington of Brumfield Parish, Culpeper County, planter, to Edward Price of same, planter. Lease of 150 acres whereon Price now lives ... in the Little Fork of Rappahannock River ... being a separate parcell of a greater tract formerly granted to Edward Herndon Junr. by patent 16 June 1738 for 300 acres and conveyed by Herndon to Robert Covington ... survey made by Richard Young ... crossing a branch ... on a mountain ...
For lives of Edward Price and Euphan his wife and Rachel daughter of Edward and Euphan Price.
Annual rent 500 pounds of tobacco on 25 December (the first three years' rent excepted).
They shall work four working tithables a year and no more, Edward and Euphan and their daughter exclusive, and shall plant and keep under a good fence one hundred apple trees and shall not waste any timber.

Edward (X) Price
Robert Covington
20 March 1755. Acknowledged by the parties.
[Two indentures, one signed by each]

Pages 282-83. 17 April 1755. John Wharton of St. Mark's
Parish, Culpeper County, doth put himself an apprentice to
Jesse Harper of same, joinner, to learn his art and mistery
and to serve from the date hereof until he shall arrive to the
age of twenty one years. He shall do no damage to his master
nor see it done by others without giving notice thereof; he
shall waste his master's goods nor lend them to any; he shall
not commit fornication nor contract matrimony during the term;
he shall not play at cards, dice or any other unlawfull game;
he shall not absent himself day or night from his master's
service unlawfully nor haunt ale houses, taverns or playhouses.
His master shall teach his apprentice in the trade or mistery
he now followeth and to read and write and provide for him
sufficient meat, drink, apparel, lodging, washing and all
other necessarys and at the expiration of the term give him
£3.10.- current money.   John Wharton
                              Jesse Harper
     17 April 1755. Approved of by the Court.

Pages 283-86. 4 April 1755. Michael Holt and Elizabeth his
wife of Brumfield Parish, Culpeper County, to Jeremiah Early
of same. For £155 current money. Tract granted to Michael
Holt by patent 24 June 1726 for 400 acres ... side of a
branch of the Island Run ... another branch of the Island Run.
     Likewise 100 acres in aforesaid parish being part of a
tract granted to John Rucker by pattent ... Wm. Offill's line
... Michael Holt's line ... head of the Muddy Branch ... line
of John Rucker ...   Michael Holt
                          Eliza (X) Holt
     Wit: Jos. (X) Edins, Wm. (J) Harvey, Thos. Kirtley, Tho.
Stanton.
     17 April 1755. Acknowledged by the parties.

Pages 287-91. 14-15 April 1755. Michael Holt, Elizabeth Holt,
John Holt and Mary Holt, all of Culpeper County, to Adam Garr
of same. Lease and release; for £35 current money. 122½
acres, part of a patent granted to Michael Holt for 245 acres
28 Sept. 1728 ... in Rucker's line ... line of a patent granted
Michael Holt ... in William Eddins' line ...
                          Michael Holt
                          Elizabeth (X) Holt
                          John (X) Holt
                          Mary (X) Holt
     Wit: Jas. Barbour, Adam (AW) Wilhite, Martin (X) Rouse.
     17 April 1755. Acknowledged by the parties, Elizabeth
being first privily examined.
     17 July 1755. Acknowledged by Mary wife of John Holt.

Pages 291-92. 26 June 1756. Richard Barnes of Richmond County
Gent., to John Moreton Jordan of same, Gent. In consideration

of a marriage allready had and solemnized between John Moreton
Jordan and Elianor the daughter of Richard Barnes and love
and affection and five shillings.   1000 acres in St. Mark's
Parish, 300 acres, parcel thereof being that part of a larger
tract of land containing 1020 acres formerly purchased by
Richard Barnes of William Skrine which lies in the south side
of Flatt Run ...   300 acres, another part thereof, being formerly granted to Richard Barnes by patent 26 June 1731 ...
400 acres, the other part, being another tract formerly granted
to Richard Barnes by deed poll from the Proprietor's Office
of the Northern Neck 3 Oct. 1749 ... all which are contiguous
and adjoyning to each other.
                         Richd. Barnes
   Wit: Wm. F. Brockenbrough, John Muse, Webb Woodward, Thomas
Dolman, Michel Hart, Thoms. Brown, Jonathan Pratt, Alvin
Mountjoy.
   21 Oct. 1756.   Proved by William Francis Brockenbrough,
Webb Woodward and Jonathan Pratt.

Pages 292-95.   14 Oct. 1755.   Richard Downs of Brumfield Parish,
Culpeper County, to Mark Stowers of same.   For £24.6.8 current
money.   243 acres on Stanton River ... at the foot of
Peltram's Mountain ... Benja. Smith's line ... crossing the
run ... east side of the river ... David Jones's land ...
another tract of land that Downs sold William Stowers ... on
the river bank by a path ... crossing the river ... opposite
to the mouth of a run ... side of a mountain ...
                         Richd. Downs
   Wit: William Stowers, Saml. Canterbury, John (X) Thomson,
William (X) Sims, Joshua Early.
   16 Oct. 1755.   Acknowledged by the parties.

Pages 296-98.   20 Nov. 1755.   Christopher Holt and Elizabeth
his wife of Brumfill Parish, Culpeper County, to John Harrison
of St. Mary's Parish, Caroline County.   For £29 current money.
222½ acres in Brumfill Parish ... corner to Michael Holt
and John Broyl ... corner made by John Holt and Christopher
Holt ... given to Christopher Holt by his father Michael Holt
by deed 15 March 1754.   Christopher (O) Holt
                             Elizabeth (X) Holt
   20 Nov. 1755.   Acknowledged by the parties.
   20 Nov. 1755.   Bond of Christopher Holt of Brumfill Parish
Culpeper County, unto John Harrison of St. Mary's Parish,
Caroline County.   For £58 current money.   To fulfill all
agreements in the indenture.
                         Christopher (O) Holt
   20 Nov. 1755.   Acknowledged by Christopher.

Pages 298-99.   18 Sept. 1755.   Samuel Klug otherwise called
George Samuel Klug, Clerk, of Culpeper County, to Charles Dick
of Fredericksburg, merchant.   Mortgage to secure £74.17.11,
payable 10 June next.   Four Negro slaves, man Jethro, woman
Sarah, boy Jo alias Joseph, girl Hannah.
                         George Samuel Klug
   Wit: Thos. Landrum.

20 Nov. 1755. Acknowledged by said George Samuel [Klug].

Pages 300-01. 30 May 1755. Rowland Cornelius to Andrew Cockron, William Crawford & Co., merchants in Glasgow, North Britain. Mortgage to secure £28.9.-. Tract in the fork of Blackwater Run at the red oak Mountain bounded by the Reverend John Thompson and William Goggan. Also six Negroes, Conder, Moll, Stephen, Young Conder, Lid and Gabriel and Pennie [sic].
                                        Rowland Cornelius
    Wit: Hector Ross, James Wilson, William Cunninghame.
    20 Nov. 1755. Acknowledged by said Rowland.

Pages 301-04. 4 Nov. 1755. William Offill and Mary Offill his wife of Brumfield Parish, Culpeper County, to John Offill of same. For £10 current money. 100 acres in Brumfield Parish, being part of a patent granted formerly to John Rucker and bounded by the lines of Ephraim Rucker, Isaac Findley, Richard Vawter, Jeremiah Early and Peter Rucker.
                                        William Offill
                                        Mary Offill
    Wit: James Archer, Thomas (X) Lampton, Mary (X) Holt.
    20 Nov. 1755. Proved by James Archer, Thomas Lampton and Mary Holt.

Pages 304-11. 15-16 Oct. 1755. George Hume of Culpeper County to James Hunter of Fredericksburg, merchant. Lease and release; for £28.10.4 current money. 200 acres granted by patent 21 May 1748 to George Hume ... in John Spotswood, Esqr., line and corner to William Stanton.
                                        G. Hume
    Wit: Roger Dixon, Thos. Lendrum, Thos. Rogers.
    18 April 1755. Proved by Thomas Rogers, Thomas Lendrum and Roger Dixon.

Pages 311-14. 20-21 March 1755. Alexander Howard of Raughley Parish, Amelia County, planter, to Charles Benson of Overwharton Parish, Stafford County, planter. Lease and release; for £5 current money. 400 acres in St. Mark's Parish in the Great Fork of Rappahannock ... on the south side of a branch of Fleshman's Run ...
                                        Alexander Howard
    Wit: James Jeffries, Enoch Benson, Edward (X) Harvey, John Grant, Ann (X) Woodward.
    17 April 1755. Proved by James Jeffries, Enoch Benson and Edward Harvey.

Pages 315-17. 17 July 1755. John Jones and Catharine his wife to William Cunninghame of Falmouth, merchant. For £50 current money. 400 acres granted to Jones by the Right Honorable Thomas Lord Fairfax, Baron of Cameron in the part of Great Britain called Scotland, Proprietor of the Northern Neck of Virginia ... on the Rush River ... survey made by James Genn ... in Mr. Francis Thornton's line corner to John Lacey's tract ... on the Rush River in the Fork ... by a

great stone on a mountain side ...
>   John Jones
>   Catharine (X) Jones

   17 July 1755. Acknowledged by the parties. Catharine was first privily examined.

Pages 317-20. 28 Sept. 1755. James Pendleton and Elizabeth his wife of Culpeper County to Henry Huffman of same, weaver. For £70 current money.   250 acres in the north little fork of Rappahannock River on one of the branches of Great Indian Run call'd Willis's Run, being part of 3000 acres which James Pendleton had of John Willis of Great Britain, Esqr. ... on the east side of the branch corner of a tract surveyed for Christopher Hutchings near Huffman's corn field ... Willis's line ... branch of Indian Run ... on the ridge ...
>   James Pendleton
>   Eliza. Pendleton

   18 Sept. 1755. Acknowledged by the parties. Elizabeth was first privily examined.

Pages 320-22. 31 March 1755. Thomas Stanton of Brumfield Parish, Culpeper County, to William Harvey of same county. For £5 current money.   200 acres that fell by will to Elizabeth Stanton by Thomas Stanton, deceased, alias now Elizabeth Harvey ... on the south side of Stanton River corner to Leonard and Thomas Stanton ... on a branch ... on a ridge ... by the road ... on the river ... in Brumfield Parish, part of a patent granted to Thomas Stanton, deceased, for 400 acres 26 June 1731 ...
>   Thos. Stanton

   Wit: William Stanton, Jeremiah (J) Early, Jno. Hume, George Hume Junr.
   17 April 1755. Acknowledged by the party.

Pages 322-27. 6 Feb. 1755. Edward Dillard and Elizabeth his wife of Culpeper County to Martin Nalle of same. For £20 current money.   100 acres in the Gourd Vine Fork, part of a patent granted to William Lobb 10 Jan. 1735 ... in the low grounds of the south fork of the Gourd Vine River in or near the Reverend Mr. John Thompson's line ... near a branch ... up the river ...
>   Edward Dillard
>   Elizabeth (X) Dillard

   Wit: Fras. Slaughter, J. Pendleton, George Dillard.
   7 Feb. [1755]. Commission to Francis Slaughter, Philip Clayton and James Pendleton, Gent., to receive the acknowledgment of Elizabeth, wife of Edward Dillard.
   7 Feb. 1755. Elizabeth, wife of Edward Dillard, declared she was willing the same should be recorded.
>   Fras. Slaughter
>   J. Pendleton

   21 March 1755. Proved by James Pendleton and George Dillard.
   18 April 1755. Proved by Francis Slaughter, Gent.

Pages 327-29. 15 May 1755. Aaron Botts and Margett his wife of Culpeper County to John Gale of same. For £30 current money.

135 acres ... on a hill corner to John Gale's land and the Revd. Mr. John Thompson ... in the late Colo. Thornton's line ... corner to John Gayle ... by deed from the Proprietor's Office 4 Dec. 1751 granted to Aaron Botts.

Aaron Botts
Margett (X) Botts

Wit: Richard Nalle, John Nalle, John Duncan.
15 May 1755. Acknowledged by the parties. Margett was first privily examined.

Pages 330-33. 12 May 1754. Joseph Cotten of Culpeper County to Robert Eastham of same. For £5 current money. 400 acres ... corner to Francis Thornton and James Taylor White in the head of a valley ... hear of a valley near a branch of Thornton's River at the foot of the Oven Top Mountain ...

Joseph (J) Cotten

Wit: John (J) Lacy, Thomas (X) Riddle, Robert Deatherage, Phil. Deatherage.
15 May 1755. Acknowledged by the party.

Pages 333-35. 15 May 1755. John Gale and Sarah his wife of Culpeper County to William Reynolds of same. For £40 current money. 151 acres ... in the Gourd Vine Fork ... corner to Colo. Francis Thornton, deceased ... in the Revd. Mr. John Thompson's line ... by a branch ... corner to Thomas Poole's line ... by deed from the Proprietor's Office 1 July 1749 granted to Joseph Campbell and by Campbell conveyed to Moses Botts and by Botts was conveyed to Gayle.

John Gayle

15 May 1755. Acknowledged by the party.

Pages 336-38. 19 June 1755. Henry Field and Esther Field of St. Mark's Parish, Culpeper County, to our lawfull begotten son Henry Field. For love and effection. Two tracts, the one being the land whereon we live being the upper part of the tract for 1338 acres by deed 12 August 1748 being the upper part of the pattent ... at the mouth of a branch known by the name of the dividing branch or Roberts' Branch ... back line of the pattent ... crossing Mountain Run ... near the river bank ... containing 600 acres.
The other, 1242 acres by pattent 12 Aug. 1748 on the drains of Meandrow Run known by the name of Tenant's Church tract.

H. Field
Esther (E) Field

Wit: Danl. Brown, Wm. Brown.
19 June 1755. Acknowledged by the parties, Esther being first privily examined.

Pages 338-41. 23 May 1755. Thomas Stanton of Culpeper County to George Hume of same. For £5 current money. 204 acres that fell by will to Jane Stanton by Thomas Stanton, deceased, alias Jane Hume ... William Kirtley's line ... in Brumfield Parish ... part of a pattent granted to Thomas Stanton, deceased, for 400 acres 10 June 1737.

Thos. Stanton

Wit: William Stanton, Jeremiah (J) Early, John Hume, Wm. (HVase) Harvey.
19 June 1755. Acknowledged by the party.

Pages 341-46. 18-19 June 1755. Thomas Stanton, eldest son and heir at law to Thomas Stanton, deceased, and Lettice his wife of Culpeper County to William Stanton (second son of Thomas Stanton the father). Lease and release; for £30 and two Negroes of the value of £60 current money. Two tracts, one 684 acres on Stanton River at the Great Mountains bounded as in a patent 28 May 1751. The other 1000 acres on the lower end of the Fork of Rappahannock River bounded as in patent 30 May 1726, which tracts were devised by the will of Thomas Stanton the father to William Stanton for life only, whereby the reversion in fee of the lands became vested in Thomas Stanton as heir at law. Thos. Stanton
Lettice Stanton
Wit: H. Field, G. Hume Junr.
19 June 1755. Acknowledged by Thomas and Lettice.

Pages 346-48. 19 June 1755. Charles Kavanaugh of Culpeper County to John Conner of Orange County and Elizabeth his wife. For £10 current money. 400 acres on the branches of Muddy Run in the Fork of Rappahannock River which was by deed 5 June 1734 conveyed unto John Conner and Elizabeth his wife by Philemon Kavanaugh by deed of record in Spotsylvania County Court and all interest Charles Kavanaugh may have in the land.
Chars. Kavanaugh
Wit: John Barrow, Edward Watkins Junr., John Triplett.
19 June 1755. Acknowledged by the party.

Pages 348-49. 3 June 1755. Mosley Battaley of Spotsylvania County to my two grandchildren Battaley Bryan and Anna Bryan. For good will and natural affection.
Unto my grandson Battaley Bryan a Negro woman Phillis and her son Nate and Jacob.
Unto my grandaughter Anna Bryan a Negro girl Sarah now in the possession of my son John Battaley.
M. Battaley
Wit: Roger Dixon, Tho. Rogers, Thos. Lendrum.
19 June 1755. Proved by Roger Dixon, Thomas Rogers and Thomas Lendrum.

Pages 349-51. 6 June 1755. Colo. William Russell of Culpeper County to William Cunningham of the Town of Falmouth, King George County. Mortgage to secure £69.10.10 sterling, to be paid by 10 June next. 1000 acres in Orange County on the south side of the Rappadan River bounded as in a patent granted to William Russell 12 Jan. 1753 ... on the west side the Russel Run corner to Jonathan Gibson ... corner of Gibson's and Mungo Roy ... Dewit's line ...
W. Russell
Wit: Thos. Lendrum, John Stewart, John Mitchell, Danl. Brown.
19 June 1755. Proved by Thos. Lendrum, John Mitchell and John Stewart.

Pages 352-55. 22 May 1755. Colo. Thomas Chew and Martha Chew
his wife and Timothy Crosthwait of St. Thomas' Parish, Orange
County, to Benjamin Head of same. For £30 current money.
200 acres in Brumfield Parish, part of a tract sold by Capt.
Henry Downs 3 June 1751 unto Chew and Crosthwait ... on the
north side of the Rappadan River ... corner of Joseph Emmons
...on the west side of Maple Run ...

Thos. Chew
Timo: Crosthwait

    Wit: William (W) Goulding, Robert Sharman, Robert Sharman
Junr.
    19 June 1755. Acknowledged by Chew and proved by William
Goulding and Robert Sharman Junr.
    17 July 1755. Proved by Robert Sharman.
    26 June [1755]. Commission to Taverner Beale, Alexander
Waugh and James Madison, Gent., to take the acknowledgment of
Martha, wife of Thomas Chew.
    7 Aug. 1755. Martha, wife of Thomas Chew, Gent., declared
she was willing the same should be recorded.

Taverner Beale
James Madison

Pages 355-57. 6 June 1755. Col. Wm. Russell of Culpeper
County to William Cunningham of Falmouth, merchant. Mortgage
to secure £69.10.10 sterling, payable 10 June next.   1000
acres granted to William Russell by patent 16 June 1727 ...
at the German Run corner to Colo. Spotswood ... head of a
branch ...

W. Russell

    Wit: John Stewart, John Mitchell, Thos. Lendrum, James
Hunter.
    19 June 1755. Proved by Thomas Lendrum, John Mitchell and
John Stewart.

Pages 357-60. 28 May 1753. William Beverley of Blanfield,
in the County of Essex, Esquire, to Rice Brown of Culpeper
County, planter.   Lease of 201 acres whereon he now dwells
being part of William's tract called Wakefield ... surveyed by
Richard Young, surveyor ... on the east side of the Pass Road
near a branch ... by a thick swamp ... by a glade ... crossing
the Indian River ... by the side of a glade ... saving liberty
of making a path or rolling road through the land where it
shall be necessary for and desired by one or more tenants of
William.
    For the lives of the said Rice, Catherine his now wife and
Margaret Wilson.
    Yearly rent on 7 December a crop note of Fredericksburg
or Fallmouth Inspectors for one hogshead to contain 1000 pounds
of tobacco. If Rice shall work more than four tithables
besides himself, to pay 105 pounds of tobacco additional rent.
    He shall within two years plant one hundred apple trees
thirty feet asunder, also an orchard of good peach trees
twenty feet asunder. ...

W. Beverley

Wit: W. Russell, Robt. Coleman, Danl. Brown.
    22 Nov. 1755 [1754]. Proved by Robt. Coleman and Danl.
Brown.
    20 June 1755. Proved by William Russell, Gent.

Pages 360-64. 10 Aug. 1754. John Roberts of Brumfield Parish,
Culpeper County, and Elizabeth his wife to James Slown of
St. Mark's Parish, Culpeper County.   For £20 current money.
289 acres being the lowermost part of a greater tract granted
to John Roberts by the Proprietor of the Northern Neck 18 June
1748 for 589 acres, the uppermost part whereof was formerly
conveyed by John Roberts to Richard Young ... in the Little
Fork of Rappahannock River and joining to Battle Mountain ...
on a branch ... corner of Richard Young ...
                         John (J) Roberts
                         Elizabeth (E) Roberts
    Wit: William Johnson Junr., William Roberts, Ander. (A)
Horrish.
    17 July 1755. Acknowledged by John Roberts and Elizabeth
his wife.

Abbet, Elizabeth (   )   16
   Roger   16
   Waddington   16-17
   William   16-17
Abell, Joseph   18
Albemarle Co., Va.   1
Amburger, Conrad   19, 30
Amelia Co., Va.   79
Amelia Road   39
Amiss, Joseph   16
Anderson, Jeorge   59
   James   36, 40
Archer, James   49, 53, 79
Armistead, William   68
Asher, Charles   47
   John   18, 47, 49
   Moley   47
Ashley, ---   31
   John   40, 42, 45, 53
Augusta Co., Va.   25, 31
Autuback, Henry   31
   see also Utterback
Ayler, Henry   28

Back, Hamon   64
Baker, Thomas   29, 58, 66
Bakmer, Herman   5
Ball, Armistead   5
   Samuel   67
   W.   24
Ballard, Bland   19, 60
Banks, Adam   42-43
   Gerard   43
   Rosana (   )   42-43
Barbour [Barber], James
        18, 22, 60, 77
Barksdell, William   29-30
Barler, Christopher   45
   Jacob   4, 45
   Mary (   )   45
   Matthias   17, 49
Barnes, Elianor   78
   Richard   1, 74, 77-78
Barnett, ---   76
   James   12
Barns, John   29, 58
Barrow, John   25, 82
Bates, William   71
Battaile, Nicholas   26, 58
Battaley, Elizabeth (   )
     Taliaferro   6-7, 39, 56
    John 22, 47, 53, 56, 62, 82
    Moseley   6, 21, 39, 56, 82
    Samuel   22
                 84

Battle Mountain   39, 84
   see also Little Battle
     Mountain
Battle Run 31, 39, 42, 45, 52
   see also Little Battle Run
    Great Battle Run
Baylor, John   28
Beale, Taverner   1, 83
Beautiful Run   13, 61
Beaver Branch   4
Beaverdam Run   4, 25, 32
Belfield, John   1
   Mary (   )   1
   Thomas Wright   1, 70
Bell, John   51
Benger, Elliott   20-21, 33
   36-38, 44, 47, 63-64, 68
Benson, Charles   79
   Enoch   79
Bernard, R.   56
Berryman, Benjamin   53
   John   53
   Mary (   )   53
   Maximilian   53
Besse Bell Mountain   1
Beverley, William   9, 15-16
   41, 50-52, 63, 65-67, 83
Beyerbeck, Frederick   28
Blackwater Run   78
Blancumbeker, Matthew   22
Blandfield, Essex Co.
   15-16, 50, 63, 65-66, 83
Blankenbeker, Christopher   45
Blankinbecker, Zach: 12
Bledsoe, Moses   49
   William   60
Blewford, John   62
Bloodworth, Joseph 19, 30, 39
Bloodworth's Road
       21, 37, 70, 74
Blue Ridge Mountains   25
Blushes Bluff   73
   see also Bushes Bluff
Bobo, Mary (   )   4
   Spencer   4, 12, 18
Bohannon, Ambrose   62
   Bathsheba (   )   56
   Elliot   62
   Robert   56
Bond, Elizabeth   8
   John   8
   Mary   8
   Mary (   )   8
Booton, William   61-62

Botts, Aaron   80-81
    Margett (   )   80-81
    Moses   4, 34, 81
Bourn, Andrew   50
Bow, see Burs
Boyer, John   6
Bramham, John   7-9, 64
Brashers, Philip   42
Breeding, Abner   49
    Ann   49
    Druscilla   49
    Elijah   49
    Job   49
    Ossamon   49
    Richard   49
Brockenbrough, William Francis
                                   78
Broil, Courtly   65
    Jacob   58
    Margaret (   )   65
    see also Broyl
Bromfield Parish
            41-42, 45, 49, 52
          56-57, 60, 62, 64-65
        67-68, 72, 74-81, 83-84
Brooke, Robert   63
Brooking, Charles   76
Brown, Anna (   )   30, 48
    Catherine (   )   83
    Coleman   30-31, 48
    Daniel   2, 7, 18, 20-21
          38, 40, 43, 46-47, 49
          61, 67-69, 81-82, 84
    Edward   36
    Eleanor (   )   25
    Frances (   )   2, 7
    Francis   30, 48
    Jane (   )   36
    John   19, 36, 75
    Rice   83
    Thomas   25-26, 41, 47, 78
    William   17, 42, 69, 81
Browning, Frances (   ) 42, 45
    Francis   2-3, 14, 20
          31, 42, 45-46, 52
    John   42
    Nicholas   3, 14
Broyl, Adam   46, 69
    Jacob   61
    John   60, 78
    see also Broil
Bruce, George   24-25
    John   22-23
Brunswick Parish, King George
        Co., Va.   11

Bryan, Anna   82
    Battaley   82
    Richard   6, 39
Buck Run   33
Buckner, Richard   3, 28
    Thomas   27, 29, 73, 75
Buford, John   24
Bullard, Ambrose   34
Burdyne's Run   57
Burgess, ---   41
Burgess River   65-66
Burgis, Thomas   38
Burk, John   23
Burke, Richard   41
Burs, Tomitz   19
Burton, Hannah (   )   76
    May   76
Bushes Bluff   29, 75
    see also Blushes Bluff
Butler, Walter   15, 43, 59
Butler's Swamp   32
Butten [Button], John 4, 6, 31
Buttock Run   19

Cabin Branch   2, 11, 14
Cabler, Frederick   39
Cage, Samuel   14
Cameron, Baron of, see
        Fairfax, Thomas, Lord
Campbell, Alexander
                       17, 56, 70
    Daniel   17, 32-33, 44, 70
    Joseph   4, 34, 81
    Sarah (   )   4
Cannon's River   62-63
Canterbury, Samuel   78
Caroline Co., Va.   5, 15, 18
        26-30, 45, 58, 71-72, 78
Carpenter, Barbara (   )   22
    John   22, 28
Carr, William   68-69
Carter, Col. ---
                   17, 32, 51, 56
    Robert   40
Carter's Run   51
Cassler, Frederick   15
Castler [Casler], Matthias
                       17, 27, 65
Catlett, Col. John   3
Cattail Branch   24
Cave, David   38
    Robert   60-62, 68
Cave's Road   62
Cedar Run   34-35, 64
Chambers, Elizabeth (   )   33

Chambers, Thomas 33
Champe, John 44
Charles Co., Md. 50
Chesterfield Co., Va. 40
Chestnut Branch 23, 41, 50
Chew, Martha ( ) 83
Thomas 9, 35, 40, 83
Chiles, William 65
Chism, --- 32
Chissam, --- 17
Chisum, John 4
Chizem, --- 56
Choice, Anne ( ) 13, 36
Tully 13, 36
Christopher, Anne ( ) 39
John 6, 39
Morton 64
William 63-64
Christy, Julius 68-69
Clar, Michael 64
see also Clore, Glore
Clayton, Ann ( ) 7-8, 15, 43
Philip 2, 5, 7-9
15, 17, 25-28, 31-32
34-35, 40-41, 43-44
59, 61, 64, 66-67, 69, 80
Samuel 34-35
Clayton's Mill Pond 44
Clore, John 26-27, 73
Michael 26
see also Clar, Glore
Cockron, Andrew, William
Crawford & Co. 79
Cofer [Coffer], Thomas
10, 59, 71
Coleman, Robert 7, 12, 17-18
21, 25, 32, 34-35, 42, 44
47, 59, 64, 66-69, 74, 84
Samuel 30
Sarah ( ) 18
Compton, Capt. --- 22, 29
Connor, Elizabeth ( ) 82
James 58
John 82
Conway, --- 10
Francis 42
Conway River 29, 73
Cook, Michael 22, 28
Shem 38
Cooper, Abraham 14, 20, 41
John 20, 23, 42
Joseph 67
Judith ( ) 20
Copland's Run 64
Corbin, Elizabeth (Scott) 23

Corbin, Thomas 23, 41
Cornelius, Rowland 7, 18, 79
Cotten, James 19, 58
Joseph 58, 81
Sarah ( ) 19
Counce, Joseph 4
Courthouse Road 20, 37, 59
Covington, Elizabeth ( ) 70
Robert 7, 28-29, 76-77
Thomas 5, 8, 70
William 7, 29
Cowne, William 15, 32, 43
Cox, Francis 7
Cragg, Taliaferro 34
Crawford, --- 12
John 16, 52
Reuben 16
Thomas 60
William 16, 60, 79
Crease, Lawrence 65
Crigler, Nicholas 64
see also Krugler
Crim, --- 17, 32
Crimb, John 31
Crittenden, Eleanor ( ) 13
John 72
William 13
Crooked Run 50
Crosthwait, Timothy 35, 83
William 40
Crump, John 55, 75
Cummerford, James 53
Cunningham, William
32, 56, 70, 79, 82-83

Dandridge, Dorothea
(Spotswood) 21, 44, 68
Nathaniel West 21, 44, 68
Daniel, Vivion 75
Dark Run 18
Davis [Davies], David 12, 53
Day, John 37
Deatheridge, --- 17, 32, 56
William 4
Deatherage, Phil. 81
Robert 81
Deatherage's Run 72-73
Deep Run 30, 67
Deer, John 37, 48
Delamore forest tract 6
Deleny, John 31
Delph, Conrad 63
Dent, John 58
Dewitt, --- 32, 56, 82
Charles 3-4, 6

Dewitt, Joseph   17-18
    Martin   14, 19, 31
    Mary (   )   31
    see also Duett
Dick, Charles   6, 9-10
              21, 34-35, 46, 78
Dickerson, Nathaniel   13
Dillard, Edward   3, 27, 80
    Elizabeth (   )   80
    George
          11, 27, 31, 38, 74, 80
    James   50
    John   50
    Thomas   8-9, 11-12, 27, 31
    Winifred (   )   11-12
Dixon, ---   60
    Roger   5-6, 8-9, 11, 17
         26-30, 37, 41, 43-45, 47
         55=56, 58, 68-69, 79, 82
Doggett, Thomas   39
Dogwood Branch   19
Dolman, Thomas   78
Donne, Samuel   44
Dougharty, Edward   23
    John   23
Dovel's Run   30
Dowdy, Elizabeth (   )   48
    John   48
Downer, Moses   41
    Thomas   62, 68
Downer's Path   62
Downs, ---   71
    Henry   12-13, 19, 24-25
         31, 35-36, 62, 69, 83
    Jane (   )   13
    Richard   70, 78
Dozier, Leonard   64
Dragon Run   30
Duckworth, Thomas   61
Duett, Charles   31
    see also Dewitt
Duett's Road   72
Duff, William   1, 13, 36, 43
Duncan, ---   3
    John   46, 81
    Rowly   1
    William   1, 20, 46, 59
Durrett, John   15, 41, 43
    Mary (   )   41
    Richard   41
Duvall, Daniel   72

Early, Jeremiah   14, 46
         56-57, 70, 77, 79-80, 82
    John   57

Early, Joshua   78
Eastham, George   19, 59, 74
    John   73
    Robert   11-12, 31-32
         38, 50, 61, 73, 81
    William   37, 73
Eddins, Abraham   14, 28
    John   56
    Joseph   57, 77
    Mary (Stanton)   57
    William   56, 61, 74, 77
Edmonds, Elias   51-52, 75
    William   51-52
Edwards, Charles   51
Elk Run   59-60
Elkwood, Culpeper Co. 16, 51
Elly, Henry   74
Emmons, Joseph   83
Essex Co., Va.
          9-10, 15-16, 37, 41
         44, 50, 63, 65-66, 83

Fairfax, Bryan   15, 43
    George   22, 25
    Thomas   25
    Thomas, Lord
         5, 11, 15, 20, 26, 29
         41, 43, 50, 56, 61, 79
    William Henry   15, 43
Fairfax Co., Va.   34
Falmouth, Va. 65-66, 79, 82-83
Falmouth Warehouse   51, 63
Fargeson, B.   17
Farguson, Samuel   18
Farmer, Daniel   51
    John   46, 50-51
    Mary (   )   51
Farrow's Run   14
Faver [Favour], ---   35
    John   7-8, 59
Field, Abraham   1, 37, 45
    Daniel   51
    Esther (   )   81
    Henry   1, 6, 8, 24-25
         33, 35, 39-40, 43
         51, 68-69, 74, 81-82
    John   41, 48-49, 53
Findley, Isaac   79
Finlason, ---   30
Finnell [Finnal], Jonathan
                          62, 68
    Mary (   )   68
    Thomas   9
Finney, ---   25
Finnie, James   12

Fishback, ---   17, 32, 56
   Anaelizabeth ( )   31-32
   Frederick
     4, 18, 31-32, 72-73
Fisher, Ludwig   58
Fitzgerald, Walter 6, 21-22, 39
Fitzhugh, Daniel   70
   John   32
   Thomas   32, 56
Flat Run   5, 24, 29, 48, 78
Fleshman, Ciriaces [Seraicas]
     57-58, 61
   John   57
   Peter   57-58, 61
Fleshman's Run   79
Floury, Daniel   66
   Martha ( )   66
Fox Mountain Tract   5, 70
Foxe, ---   63
Fredericksburg, Va. 9, 11, 14
     23, 65-67, 78-79, 83
Freeman, Robert   8
   Thomas   74
Freeman's Mill Run   8
French, Hugh   26
Frogg, Elizabeth ( ) 55, 75
   John   11, 41-42, 55, 75
Froggit, Robert   14-15, 27
Fry, Joshua   7

Gaines, Francis   34
   William   44
Gale, John   80-81
   Sarah ( )   81
   see also Gayle
Gambill, Henry   61, 66
   Mary ( )   66
Garnett, Capt. Anthony   46
Garr, Adam   77
   Lawrence   22
Garrett, Matthew   30
Garrot, Thomas   7
Garth's Run   14, 75
Garth's Spring   71
Garton, Uriah   41
Gayle, John   34, 49-50, 81
   see also Gale
Gear, Nathaniel   72
General Court   36
Genn, James   79
George, John   41, 45
German old lot   47
German Road   30, 67
German Run   83
Gett, John   15-16

Gett, Stephen   15
   see also Jett
Giant's Castle Mountain   12
Gibson, Jonathan   30, 82
Gillison, James   30
   John   30
Glasgow, Scotland   79
Glebe   40
Glore, Barbara ( )   19
   George   19
   Michael   19, 64
   Peter   64
   see also Clar, Clore
Gloucester Co., Va.   68
Goggan, William   18, 79
Gosney, William   64
Gouge, Benjamin   65
   John   65
   Mary ( )   65
Goulding, William   83
Gourdvine Fork   3-4, 7
     26, 34, 75, 80-81
Gourdvine River   2-3, 12
     14, 19-20, 50, 75, 80
Grant, John   22, 79
Grasty, Sharshall   74
Graves, James   11, 58
   Thomas   11, 43
Great Battle Run   39
   see also Battle Run
Great Fork, Rappahannock
     River 1-3, 26, 30, 39-41
     49-50, 59, 67, 74, 79
Great Indian Run   63, 80
   see also Indian Run
Great Mountains
     25, 36, 40, 75, 82
Green, ---   17, 32
   Duff   2, 41
   John   50
   Robert   1-2, 7
     24, 32, 48, 50, 72
   William
     1-2, 5, 23, 28-30, 34
     41, 48, 53, 55-56, 72
Green's and Moore's Mountain
     30, 48
Griffin, David   36
   Margaret   38, 44
   Thomas   73
   William   40
Grindstone Mountain   50
Grymes, Benjamin   49
   Elizabeth   43
   Col. John   72, 76

Grymes, Richard 43
   Thomas 43
Grymes' Run 76

Hackley, John 39
Hall, John 67
Ham, Joseph 57
Hamilton Parish, Prince
    William Co.
       11, 27, 51, 53, 75
Haniker, Simon 73
Hanm, Edward 72
Hannon, Thomas 12
Harding, Charles 63
Harding, George 63
Harper, Jesse 77
Harris, David 61-62
   William 6, 32-33
Harrison, Frances ( ) 62
   John 58, 78
   Robert 62
   Thomas 41, 55
Hart, Michel 78
Harvey, Edward 79
   Elizabeth (Stanton) 80
   Francis 57
   William 77, 80, 82
Harvie, Francis 57
Hay Stack Branch 35
Haynie, Spencer 57
Hazel River 26, 30, 48, 50, 75
Head, Anthony 36, 53
   Benjamin 83
Hedgman River 16, 22, 41, 66
Henderson, Alexander 72
   John 53
   William 14, 19
      24, 28, 49, 60, 70
Henning, Samuel 70, 74
Hensley, Jane ( ) 12
   William 12
Herndon, David 28
   Edward 22, 76
   James 31
   Mary ( ) 28
Hernsberger, Stephen 5
Hickman, --- 42, 45
Hildrup, Elizabeth ( )
         9-10, 14
   Samuel 9-10, 14
Hill, Robert 23
   Russell 42, 67
Hillin, Nathaniel 42
Hinson, Joseph 32
Hole Run 30, 48

Holt, Christopher 60, 78
   Elizabeth ( ) 77-78
   John 60, 77-78
   Mary ( ) 77, 79
   Michael 19, 60, 70, 77-78
   Nicholas 57, 65
Holtzclaw, Catherine ( ) 64
   Harmon 4
   Jacob 64, 73
Home, George 30
   see also Hoome, Hume
Homes, Christopher 74
Hoome, George 5
   see also Home, Hume
Hopper, Thomas 63
Hord, Thomas 32
Horrish, Ander. 84
Horsnell, James 18, 30, 49
Houchins, see Hutchins
Houison, Thomas 34
Howard, Alexander 30, 79
Howel, Thomas 38
Hudson, Rush 9
Huffman, Henry 64, 80
   John 12, 27
Hughes' River 1, 43, 72
Hughs, John 26
Hume, Francis 74
   George 4, 6, 15, 18
     26, 47, 55, 59, 61
     64, 70, 73-74, 79-82
   James 55
   Jane (Stanton) 81
   John 80, 82
   Sarah ( ) 55
   William 55
   see also Home, Hoome
Hungry Run 70
Hunter, James 23, 67, 79, 83
   William 6-7, 21, 23, 34, 46
Hurt, James 33
Hutchins, Christopher
      8, 17, 52, 80
   Elizabeth ( ) 17
   Robert 12

Indian Run
    4, 11, 33, 52, 80, 83
   see also Great Indian Run
Isbell, James 68-69
Island Run 4, 46, 77

Jackson, David 13
   Isaac 13
   John 50

Jackson, Robert   6-7
        21, 44, 46, 58, 68-69
    Thomas   12-13, 60
    William   70
Jager, Adam   5
    see also Yager
James, Joseph   36, 67
Jeffries, James   79
Jett, James   15
    John   52, 72-73
        Sarah (Tapp)   72-73
    see also Gett
Jobbers Mountain   22
Johnson, James   19, 75
    Peter   48-49
    Valentine   19
    William   84
Johnston, Robert   37
    Seth   69
Jones, Mrs. ---   32
    Catherine (   )   40, 79-80
    David   27-28, 70, 75, 78
    Gabriel   16-17, 50, 52
    John   79-80
    Lucy   52
    Mary (   )   50
    Robert   58
    Thomas   7, 12-13, 40, 64
    William   51-52
Jordan, Elianor (Barnes)   78
    John Moreton   77-78
    William   1

Kafer, Michael   46
Kamper, Peter   31-32
Kanitzer, see Haniker
Kavanaugh, ---   17, 38, 74
    Ann (   )   47
    Charles   25, 47, 82
    Philemon   11, 47, 82
Kelly, ---   38, 74
    John   73
    William   15, 17
Kemper, see Kamper
Kendal, Henry   4
Kendrick, Jacob   15
    see also Kindrick
Kennerley, Elizabeth (   )   72
    James   30, 45, 61, 66, 72
    Mary Margaret (   )
                        6, 30, 61
    Thomas   6, 29-30, 61, 66
Kennerley's Great Branch
                           29, 61
Kennerley's Mountain 29, 45, 72

Key, Robert   29, 75
Kindrick, Jacob   39
    see also Kendrick
King and Queen Co., Va.
               20, 34, 56, 73
King George Co., Va.
    1, 11, 17, 32, 39, 41-42
        44, 51, 56, 67, 70, 75
King William Co., Va.
           15, 21, 43-44, 68
Kinkead, David   1
    Winifred (   )   1
Kinkead's Run   1
Kirker, Andreas   27
Kirtley [Kirtlet], ---
               10-11, 15, 31
    Francis   4, 6-7
        13-14, 26, 31, 38, 74
    James   74
    Margaret (   )   26
    Sary (   )   4
    Thomas   75, 77
    William   4, 57, 75, 81
Klug, George Samuel   78-79
Knight, John   64
    Matthew   64
Knox, John   32
Krugler, Christopher   28
    Jacob   28
    see also Crigler
Kuch, see Cook

Lacy, Anne (   )   26
    John   26, 79, 81
Lampton, Thomas   79
Lancaster Co., Pa.   23
Lancaster Co., Va.   51
Landrum, ---   72
    see also Lendrum
Latham, John   11, 26, 31
Lauter, Michael   62
Lawless, Michael   27
Layton, John   76
Leavell, John   64
    Robert   40
Lendrum, Thomas
               65, 70, 79, 82-83
    see also Landrum
Lewis, Fielding   6, 9-10, 21
    Henry   70
    J.   30, 47, 65, 71
    Mutton   67
    Zachary   65, 69-71
Lick Branch   57
Lightfoot, ---   37

Lightfoot, Goodrich   3, 7
            9, 15, 23, 64, 74
    Susannah (   )   7, 15
    William   24
Limestone landing   47
Lindsey, John   45
Lines, Robert   47
Little Battle Mountain   5
    see also Battle Mountain
Little Battle Run   5
    see also Battle Run
Little Fork, Rapidan River
                          22, 60
Little Fork, Rappahannock
        River   2, 5
        8, 11-12, 22-23, 28
       31, 33, 39, 41, 52, 62
       64-65, 72, 76, 80, 84
Lobb, Catherine (   )   3, 75
    William   3, 50, 75, 80
Long, Benjamin   8
    Bloomfield   8
    Elizabeth (Bond)   8
    George   17, 27, 65
    Mary (Bond)   8
    Rebecca (   )   27
Long Branch   12
Long Mountain   52
Long's Ford   17
Lost Mountain   12, 40, 76
Louisa Co., Va.   13, 75
Loury, Robert   42
Loyns, Robert   23-24
Lunenburg Parish, Richmond
        Co., Va.   18
Lynn, William   9-10, 23, 69

McDaniel, John   70
McDonaugh, William   36, 40
Macginis, James   73
McKenny, John   46
McKenzie, Malcolm   39
    Michael   62-63
Mackie, Robert   60
McQueen, Alexander
            8, 33, 58, 74-75
    John   75
McWilliams, William   44
Madison, James   1, 83
Manspoil, Ann (   )   37-38
    John   37-38
Manspoille, Jacob   12
Manyfield, John   26
Maple Run   24, 83
Martin, Zachariah   25

Marye, William   23
Massey, Charles   23
Mauldin, Richard
            1, 7, 18, 25, 40
Mayer, George   58
Mayfield, Alexander   34
Mazey, Richard   53
Meander Run   74, 81
Medley, Elizabeth (   )   76
    Jacob   76
    John   12, 76
Meely, Guy   65
Micall, Francis   18
Michals, Francis   49
Middle Run   46
Mingee, John   51
Minor, John   29, 61, 66
Mitchel, Cornelius   2
Mitchell, John   70, 82-83
Molspy, see Manspoil
Moore, Anna Catherine
        (Spotswood) 21, 44, 68
    Bernard   21, 44, 68
    Francis   9
    Harbin   34
    Samuel   50
Morpus, John   48
Mount Delamore   72
Mountain Run   3, 5, 25-26
            35, 44, 53, 69, 81
Mountjoy, Alvin   78
Moyer, Christopher   46
    George   19, 46-47, 63, 69
    Henry Mickle   58
Muddy Branch   77
Muddy Run
        11, 17, 38, 47, 74, 82
Muddy Run Mountain 15, 41, 43
Mulheir, Elizabeth (   )   48
    John   30, 48
Muse, John   78

Nalle, John   50, 81
    Martin   49-50, 75, 80
    Nathan   8-9, 42, 44-45
    Richard   11, 33, 81
Nalle's Mill   50
Nash, Betty (   )   18
    William   18, 20, 37, 49
Neal, Charles   14, 19, 31
    Hesther (   )   31
    Mary (   )   9
    William   9
Neal's Mountain   19, 31
Negro Run   6

Nicholas, John 4
Nicholson, John 44
   Mary ( ) 43-44
   Thomas 43-44
   William 26
Norman, Courtney 42, 45
   Isaac 24, 42
   Joseph 31
   Mary ( ) 42
   Sarah ( ) 31
North, Anthony 27
   Mary 27
North River 32
Northumberland Co., Va. 6

Offill, John 74, 79
   Mary ( ) 79
   William 38-39, 77, 79
Oneal, Michael 64
Orange Co., Va. 1-2
   4, 6, 9, 11-13, 20, 24
   27, 30-31, 33-37, 39-40
   44, 46-48, 51, 59-63, 65
   67-68, 70, 72-75, 82-83
Orange Old Court House 39
Oven Top Mountain 81
Overwharton Parish, Stafford
   Co., Va. 79
Owel, Christopher 75
Owens, Margaret 43
Oxford, Roger 51

Pannell [Pannil], Samuel 45
   William 3, 45, 47
Parker, --- 47
Parks, John 7-8, 59, 69
   Mary (North) 27, 38
   Richard 59
   Samuel 8-9, 17, 27, 38
   Thomas 8
Parks' Branch 35, 59
Partridge, Matthew 6
   Richard 6
Pass Run 22, 70, 83
Payton, Henry 55
Peaked Mountain 45
Peaked Mountain Road 23
Pearce, Jeremiah 74
Pearson, Michael 14
   William 14
Peirson, Charles 57
   William 57
Pellam, William 24
Peltram's Mountain 78
Pendleton, Ben 34

Pendleton, Elizabeth ( )
   2, 25, 50, 80
   James 2, 5, 25, 31
   39, 41, 50, 59, 61, 80
   Nathaniel 50, 64
   William 62
Penn, John 49
Perkins, Elisha 1
Petty, Christopher 46
Phillips, William 62
Phillips' Spring Branch 62
Pickett, --- 32
   Micajah 75
Pillow, John 71
Poe, Lydia ( ) 2, 66
   William 2, 41, 44-45, 66
Poiner, Thomas 67
Pollard, James 18, 30, 49
   Richard 64, 74
   Thomas 49
   William 49
Poole, Micajah 23
   Thomas 49-50, 81
Potato Run 15
Pound, William 9
Powell, Ambrose 7, 9
   18, 22, 25, 40, 67
   Benjamin 10, 18, 22
   Elias 69-70, 75
   James 70
   Janny ( ) 29
   John 29, 42, 73-75
   Mary ( ) 74-75
Pratt, Jonathan 40, 78
Price, Calem 12, 31
   Edward 76-77
   Euphan ( ) 76
   Mary Ann ( ) 31
   Rachel 76
Prince William Co., Va.
   5, 11, 27, 31-32, 41-42
   51=53, 55, 64, 75

Quarles, John 40
Quinn, Darby 24
   Richard 24-25

Raccoon Ford 49
Ragged Mountain 32, 72
Raines, Allin 62
Rains, James 24
Raleigh Parish, Amelia Co. 79
Rapidan River 4, 6, 9
   12-14, 17, 19, 22-24
   28, 31, 33, 36, 39, 46-47
   49, 53, 60, 64, 72, 82-83

Rappahannock River   1-3
        5, 8, 11, 13, 22-23
        26, 28, 30-31, 33, 36
        39-41, 43-44, 47, 49-52
        55, 59, 62, 64, 67-68
        72, 74, 76, 79-80, 82, 84
Rawson, John   37
Read, John   24, 33-34, 47
    Theophilus   33
    Winefred (   )   24
Read's Spring Branch   48
Red Oak Mountain 30, 46, 48, 79
Rennolds, John   7-8, 25
Reynolds, John   59
    William   81
Richmond Co., Va.
    1, 18, 24-26, 32, 74, 77
Riddle, Thomas   81
Ridley, Thomas   38
Roan, Capt. ---   30
Roberts, Benjamin   15, 39
    Elizabeth (   )   5, 84
    Jean (   )   62
    John   1, 5, 39, 42, 63, 84
    William   39, 59, 62-63, 84
Roberts' Branch   81
Robertson, Mary (   )   53
    William   53, 74
Robinson River   4, 7, 12
    17, 19, 25, 27-28, 36, 40
    46, 55, 60, 65, 70-71, 75
Rock Hall   4
Rocky Run   24, 65
Rodgers, John   31
Rogers, Thomas 56, 67, 79, 82
Rootes, Philip
        20, 38, 60, 73, 75
Rose, Rev. Robert   21, 33
        36-38, 44, 63-64, 68
Ross, Hector   79
Rosse, Andrew   17, 32
Rosson, Joseph   51, 74
Rouse, Martin   77
Roush, Matthias   12
Row, George   55, 60, 70
Rowland, Edward   1
Roy, Mungo   82
Rucker, ---   77
    Ambrose   61-62
    Cornelius   36
    Ephraim   10-11, 38, 69, 79
    Honour (   )   10
    James 12-14, 38, 42, 61-62
    John   56, 74, 77, 79
    Margaret   38

Rucker, Margaret (Vawter)
                        10-11
    Peter   38, 79
    Thomas 19, 36, 38, 42, 74
    William   10, 12-13, 38
Rumsey's Branch   49
Rush, Benjamin   60, 73
    James   73
    John   73
    Rachel (   )   73
    William   60, 73
Rush River   6-7
        26, 29, 45, 61, 79
Russell, Michael   17
    Peter   46, 67
    William   14, 16-17, 24-35
        37, 41, 51, 66-67, 82-84
Russell Run   82
Ryner, Christian   22
    Eberhart   22

St. Anne's Parish, Albemarle
    Co., Va.   1
St. George's Parish, Spotsyl-
    vania Co., Va.
                5, 11, 39-40
St. Margaret's Parish,
    Caroline Co.   5, 71
St. Margaret's Parish, Spot-
    sylvania Co.   13
St. Mark's Parish   1, 3-5
        7-9, 12, 14, 17-22
        25-28, 30, 33-36, 38-40
        44, 46-49, 53, 63, 67-69
        72, 74-75, 77-78, 81, 84
St. Mary's Parish, Louisa
    Co., Va.   13
St. Mary's Parish, Caroline
    Co., Va.   26, 29, 78
St. Thomas Parish, Orange and
    Culpeper cos.   10
        12-13, 18-19, 24, 29
        31, 36-37, 40, 60, 83
Sampson, John   53
Samuel, Giles   29
Sanders, Frances (   )   32
    John Wynall
        4, 17, 32, 38, 67
Sawyer, William   38
Scales, Richard   1
Schoolhouse Path   37
Scott, Anthony   23, 41
    Elizabeth   23, 71-72
    John   71-73
    Johnny   72

Scott, Mary 72
    Samuel 1, 42, 46
    Thomas 19, 72
Seal, Anthony 55
Shackleford, John 8, 11, 33-34
Shafer, John 58, 61
    Mary (   ) 61
Sharman, Robert 10, 83
Shaw, John Asher 41
Shedden, Robert 11
Sheperd, Andrew 60
Shirsh, Martin 27
Shoemate, John 33
Simpson, Abraham 22
    John 4, 15, 19, 32, 57
    Samuel 22
Sims, William 78
Simson, Silent 43
Skinker, Thomas 23
Skrine, William 78
Slaughter, Francis 5, 12, 24-25
        28-30, 46, 48, 53, 80
    George 63
    Robert 1, 5, 8, 17, 24
        34-35, 48, 53, 55-56
    Thomas 4-5, 18
Slown, James 84
Sluchter, Henry 58
Smith, Augustine 3, 51
    Benjamin 71, 78
    Isaac 13, 61-62
        65, 70-71, 75
    James 27
    John 3, 9, 14, 20, 42
    Margaret (   ) 61-62, 70-71
    Matthew 4-5
    Matthias 17, 45, 49
    Nicholas 17
    Robert 9
    Sarah 27
    Thomas 36, 40
Smith's Run 61-62
Snyder, Philip 28
Spada Run 47
Sparks, Mary (   ) 25
    Thomas 18, 25, 67
    William 18
Spencer, Edward 35
Spignal Hollow 32
Spilman, Jacob 64, 66-67
    James 63
Spotswood, Alexander
        20-21, 33-38, 44, 46-47
        48-49, 63-64, 68-69

Spotswood, Anna Catherina
        20-21, 37, 44, 68
    Butler (   ) 20, 33
        36-37, 44, 63-64, 68
    Dorothea 20-21, 37, 44, 68
    John 5, 7, 18, 20-21
        33-37, 44-46, 48-49, 59
        63, 68-70, 74, 79, 83
    Mary (   ) 20-21, 34-35
        44-46, 48-49, 68-69
    Robert 5, 20
        37-38, 44, 63, 68
Spotsylvania Co., Va.
        5-6, 11, 20-23
        29=30, 33-41, 44, 46-49
        64-66, 68-71, 74, 82
Spotsylvania Tract, Culpeper
    Co. 33, 36, 47, 63-64
Stafford Co., Va. 32, 56, 79
Stanton, --- 10
    Elizabeth 65, 80
    Jane 81
    John 56
    Leonard 42-43
    Lettice (   ) 56-57, 82
    Mary 57
    Mary (   ) Neal 9
    Matthew 9, 19
    Thomas 4, 14-15
        28, 42-43, 56-57, 65
        70-71, 75, 77, 80-82
    William 25, 49
        65, 71, 74, 79-80, 82
Stanton River
    4, 14-15, 27, 31, 42, 65
        69-71, 73, 78, 80, 82
Stephen, Adam 14
Stevens, James 39
    Joseph 5
    William 70
Stewart, John 82-83
Stockdale, Philip 10
Stonehouse, Thomas 26
Stone Syffer, John 12
Stony Mountain 71
Stony Run 4, 41
Stowers, Mark 70, 78
    William 78
Stratton Major Parish, King
    and Queen Co. 73
Stringfellow, Henry 52
    William 52
Strother, --- 61
    Anthony
        5, 21, 34-35, 44-45, 60

Strother, Charles 18
 Christopher 26
 Francis 14, 28-29, 66
 James 66-67
 John 7, 29
 Martha (   ) Flourey 66-67
 Mary (   ) 29
 Mildred (   ) 3
 Susanna (   ) 29
 William 3, 7, 11-12, 42, 46
Stuart, Charles 30
 Mary (   ) 39-40
 Robert 39-40
Sullenger, Elizabeth (   ) 73
 James 29
 Peter 29, 73
Sutton, Beaumont 13, 40
 John 12, 37

Tadbock, Thomas 72
Taliaferro, Elizabeth 9, 14, 56
 Elizabeth (   ) 56
 Mary 9, 14
 Robert 33
 Samuel 70
 William 67
Tanner, Christopher 28
Tapp, Sarah 72-73
 Vincent 72-73
 William 11, 72-73
Taylor, John 28, 47, 64
 Zachary 36, 40
Teale [Teele], Edward 38, 70
 John 38
Tenant's Church Tract 81
Terrell, John 76
Terril, Robert 4
Thomas, Benjamin 1-2
 Betty (   ) 60, 73
 Elizabeth 2, 7-8
 Evan 32
 John 52, 60, 73
 Joseph 12-13, 32
 Katherine (   ) 2
 Richard 2, 7-8
  13, 17, 19, 25-26, 28
  32, 40, 43, 47, 61-62
 Sarah (   ) 12
Thompson, Anne 37
 Butler (   ) Spotswood
  33-34, 37, 44, 68
 Catherine (   ) 24
 George 24
 Rev. John 3-5, 18-20
  34, 36-37, 39-41
  44, 46, 68-69, 79-81

Thompson, William 37
 see also Tomson
Thompson's Branch 68
Thomson, John 78
Thornton, Frances (   ) 11
 Francis 4, 11, 26, 28
  34, 49, 58, 79, 81
 John 49, 58, 68-69
Thornton's Pass 58
Thornton's River 25, 58, 81
Thurman, John 65, 70
 Mary 70
Thurston, Seth 24-25
Tinsley, David 19
 Isaac 38-39
 Margaret (Rucker) 38
Tomson, George 59
 see also Thompson
Toole, Elizabeth (   ) 13, 36
 Matthew 13, 36
Towles, John 69, 75
 Stockly 76
Trawick [Traweek], Margery
  (   ) 26, 46
 Robert 26, 46
Triplett, John 51, 53, 82
 Lucy (   ) 53
 Nathaniel 51, 53
 Thomas 5, 51, 53
 William 51, 53
Turman, Robert 57
Turner, James 27, 52-53
 Karenhappuck (   ) 52-53
 Mary 27
 Nathan 35
Turnip Branch, see Upper
  Turnip Branch
Tutt, Richard
  2, 34, 46, 68-69, 75
 William 4, 32
Twyman, William 10, 71
 Winnefred (   ) 71
Tyler, Anne (   ) 45
 Francis 42, 45
 Henry 45

Underwood, Nathan 59, 71
Upper Turnip Branch 20
Ursulana, Culpeper Co. 63
Utterback, --- 32, 56
 see also Autuback
Utz, George 45

Vaught, John Paul 30
Vawter, Angus 10-11
 Augustine 10-11

Vawter, Bartholomew
                10-11, 42, 74
    David   74
    John   10-11
    Margaret   10
    Richard 10-11, 38-39, 67,79
Vernon, Richard   61-62, 68

Wade, James   7, 42
Waeit, Robert   74
Wakefield, Culpeper Co.
                65-66, 83
Walk, Martin   67
Walker, Charles   24-25, 69
    Edward   62
    James   62
    Thomas   4, 23
Wallace, Michael   11, 41-42
                55-56, 68-69, 75
Waller, Jacob   63
Wallis, Humphrey   11, 23, 38
        56, 58, 64, 70-71, 74
Ward, Jacob   12, 62
Washburn, John   2
    Lucy (   )   3
    Thomas   3, 14, 23
Washington Parish, Westmore-
        land Co.   62
Watkins, Edward   82
Watters, Joseph   2
Watts, Benjamin   19, 22
    Edward   19
    Elizabeth (   )   19
    Esther (   )   22
    Joel   39
    John   19
    Thomas   18, 22, 37, 39, 60
    William   15
Waugh, Alexander   35, 64, 83
    Richard   67
Wayman, George   64
Weaver, Tilman   6, 32, 67
Wells, Stephen   64
Westmoreland Co., Va.   6, 62
Wetherall, John
        18, 34-35, 43, 46
Wharton, John   77
Whatley, Michael   47
White, Daniel   35
    James   72
    James Taylor   81
    William   58
White Oak Run   18, 46, 69
Whitehaven, England   43
Whitstone Rock Branch   4

Wiatt, Thomas   52
Wiccocomico Parish, Lancaster
    Co., Va.   51
Wilder, James   48
    Mary (   )   48
Wilhite, Adam   77
    Matthias   45
    Tobias   67
Williams, Joseph   6, 32
    Robert   9
    William
        26-28, 30, 32, 34-35
        40, 43, 46, 59, 66, 69
Willis, ---   2
    Col. Henry
            5, 15, 43-44, 72
    John   5, 80
    Nanny (   )   5
Willis' Run   80
Willson, John   7
Wilson, James   23, 41, 79
    John   25
    Margaret   83
Wolfpen Branch   57
Wood, Elizabeth (Scott) 71-72
    John Scott   71-72
    Joseph   22, 30, 71-72
Woodward, Ann   79
    Webb   78
Wooten, Thomas   47
Wright, John   75

Yager, Adam   4, 69
    Elizabeth (   )   67
    Michael   65, 67
    see also Jager
Yager Run   69
Yancey, Capt. ---   50
    Elizabeth   47
    John   74-75
    Lewis Davis 11, 47, 59-60
Yarborough, Richard   7
Yellow Banks   57
Young, John   64
    Richard   5, 39-40
        43, 46, 50, 53, 63
        65-66, 72, 76, 84-84
Yowell, Christopher   52, 64
    James   52, 64
    Margaret (   )   64

Zachary, Ann (   )   19, 60
    David   60
    James   13, 60
    John   18-19, 60

Zachary, Thomas   12
Zeigler, Leonard   15
Zimmerman, Christopher   39

Heritage Books by John Frederick Dorman:

Culpeper County, Virginia Deeds, Volume One, 1749–1755
Culpeper County, Virginia Deeds, Volume Two, 1755–1762
Culpeper County, Virginia Deeds, Volume Three, 1762–1765
Culpeper County, Virginia Deeds, Volume Four, 1765–1769
Culpeper County, Virginia Deeds, Volume Five, 1769–1772

The Virginia Genealogist, Volumes 1-27
Volumes 1: 1957
Volumes 2: 1958
Volumes 3: 1959
Volumes 4: 1960
Volumes 5: 1961
Volumes 6: 1962
Volumes 7: 1963
Volumes 8: 1964
Volumes 9: 1965
Volumes 10: 1966
Volumes 11: 1967
Volumes 12: 1968
Volumes 13: 1969
Volumes 14: 1970
Volumes 15: 1971
Volumes 16: 1972
Volumes 17: 1973
Volumes 18: 1974
Volumes 19: 1975
Volumes 20: 1976
Volumes 21: 1977
Volumes 22: 1978
Volumes 23: 1979
Volumes 24: 1980
Volumes 25: 1981
Volumes 26: 1982
Volumes 27: 1983

CD-The Virginia Genealogist, Volumes 1-27